# The Retirement Specialist

## Why Retirement Requires Expertise and How to Find It

Eric T. Ludwig, Ph.D., CFP®, RICP®

STOCKBRIDGE WEALTH PRESS

ISBN: 978-1-971819-00-6

Published by Stockbridge Wealth Press

For information about special discounts for bulk purchases, please contact the author at info@stockbridgewealth.com

Publisher's Cataloging-in-Publication Data:

Names: Ludwig, Eric, 1980- author.

Title: The retirement specialist: why retirement requires different expertise and how to find it / Eric T. Ludwig, Ph.D., CFP®, RICP®

Description: First edition. | Sun Prairie, WI: Stockbridge Wealth Press, 2026.

Summary: The Retirement Specialist helps you determine whether your current advisor has specialized expertise to help you throughout retirement and how to find someone who does.

Subjects: Retirement income -- Planning. | Retirement -- Planning. | Finance, Personal. | Financial planners -- Selection. | BISAC: BUSINESS & ECONOMICS / Personal Finance / Retirement Planning.

ISBN: 978-1-971819-00-6

For Karen and Alex. I love you, girls.

# Table of Contents

# Introduction

If you're reading this, I bet you did most things right, financially.

You worked for decades, saved consistently, avoided the big financial mistakes, let compounding work its magic, and reached the moment you'd been aiming for your entire career. Retirement.

And yet, if you're honest, something still feels off.

Not because you didn't save enough. Many people reading this are in the strongest financial position of their lives. The discomfort comes from something else. It comes from the shift from building wealth to living on it.

For most of your career, your financial life had a clear direction. Paychecks showed up. Contributions flowed into retirement accounts. Market ups and downs were background noise because time was on your side.

Then one day the flow reverses.

At some point, you have to live on what you have saved. Every withdrawal feels permanent. Every market drop feels personal. You start asking questions you never had to ask before. How much can I safely spend this year? What happens if the market drops again? Which account should I pull from first? Did I claim Social Security too early? What if I live longer than expected?

These aren't academic questions. They're the ones that keep you up at night. And they shape how you live for the next thirty years of your life.

Most people assume their financial advisor will have clear answers. That assumption is where the real problem begins. I learned this the hard way.

In the fall of 2008, my office phone rang. One of my clients had recently retired and was watching his portfolio fall. Thirty percent. Forty percent. Then more. He asked a simple question.

He wanted to know if he was going to be OK. Whether he should stop spending. Whether he should sell everything. Whether his money was going to last.

I froze. I remember sitting there, staring at my screen, feeling my stomach tighten.

At the time, I had been a financial advisor for just over a year. I was twenty-eight years old. I had recently left a career as an airline pilot and been hired in September 2007, almost perfectly timed with the market peak before the financial crisis.

I was earning a master's degree in finance. I could analyze securities. I understood portfolio construction, asset allocation, and diversification. What I didn't have was an answer that solved his deceivingly simple questions.

Markets had collapsed. He was taking money out to live on. He wanted to know whether he should reduce spending, by how much, which accounts to use, whether this changed his Social Security plans, and most importantly, whether his money would still last.

I gave him the best response I had. I told him to reduce spending if possible and pull from bonds since they had held up better.

When I hung up the phone, the pit in my stomach grew. I had been trusted with someone's life savings, and I knew I wasn't prepared for what retirement income planning really demanded.

What made it worse is that this call didn't happen once. It happened again. And again. And again. People would stand outside the windows of my fishbowl of an office without an appointment, waiting desperately to get some advice. These were simply people who had done everything right for 30 years, but were now asking questions the industry never trained me to answer.

Those events changed the direction of my career. We all deal with stressful events differently. Some people are the proverbial ostrich, head in the sand, waiting for the storm to pass. I've always been more of a run-toward-the-explosion kind of person. I started obsessively studying retirement income research. Not casually reading articles. I mean nights, weekends, every spare hour. I learned quickly that the knowledge required to manage money in retirement is completely different from the knowledge used to build it.

That's when I discovered William Bengen's research that introduced what later became known as the "4% rule." It was an important starting point, but it left out major realities retirees actually face, including taxes, fees, and real-time decision-making during market crashes.

I then found research on dynamic withdrawal strategies, including guardrails that adjusted spending based on portfolio performance. It added flexibility, but again, it lived mostly on spreadsheets and backtests, not in the messy world of real people making emotional decisions under pressure.

Even when I began to understand the theory, the institution I worked for had no systems to implement it. There were no coordinated frameworks, no communication plans, and no practical playbook for helping thousands of retirees adjust spending intelligently during extreme market stress.

I talked with colleagues. Everyone was scrambling. We had all been trained essentially the same way. Broad financial knowledge across many topics, followed by the assumption that we would simply "manage" money in retirement. But *manage* usually meant doing what we had always done: rebalance portfolios, monitor performance, and maintain allocations.

Retirement introduced problems that required entirely different expertise.

That was the moment I realized this wasn't just my personal knowledge gap. It was industry-wide.

There are roughly 300,000 financial professionals in the United States. The vast majority are trained as what I would call generalists. They know something about investments, insurance, taxes, estate planning, and retirement. Breadth, not depth.

The Financial Industry Regulatory Authority (FINRA) currently lists over 252 professional designations. More than half begin with the words *Certified* or *Chartered*. And what's crazy is that *none* of them are required to legally call themselves a financial advisor.

I think anyone would agree that if you're approaching retirement and trying to figure out whether your advisor truly has the expertise needed to guide you through this phase of life, you're navigating a system that was not designed to make it easy.

How do you tell the difference between someone who helps you grow wealth versus someone who specializes in helping you live off it? Someone who can guide you through the income decisions, yes, but that's just the tip of the iceberg. There are also healthcare choices, housing questions, tax strategies, and dozens of other decisions that seemingly come at you all at once in retirement.

That's the problem this book solves.

Now, I didn't start my financial planning career intending to specialize in retirement income planning; it happened naturally, as all my first clients were retirees and near retirees. But then I realized it was the place in the financial planning arch where I could make the biggest impact, and it became my niche.

The interesting thing about working with this clientele is that it's given me front-row seats to thousands of retirements, from beginning to end. I've witnessed what works and what doesn't, and how both good decisions and bad ones compound over thirty years of retirement.

My own career path has been a curvy one. Along the way, I earned the Certified Financial Planner (CFP®) designation and left the bank environment to start Stockbridge Private Wealth Management around one singular purpose: helping people navigate the transition from accumulation to sustainable retirement income.

Fifteen years into my career, with a successful firm already built, I made a decision that raised a few eyebrows. At age forty, I went back to school to pursue a PhD in financial planning, focusing on the behavioral and psychological side of retirement. Not because I needed more designations in my title, but because I wanted deeper answers to the problems I kept seeing play out in real life.

I joined the faculty of The American College of Financial Services. Today, I teach roughly 2,000 advisors a year as a professor of Retirement Income. I direct the Retirement Income Certified Professional (RICP®) program, which provides specialized retirement income training, and I lead the Center for Retirement Income, where we conduct research on how to help Americans retire successfully.

I work with clients who need this expertise. I train advisors who serve clients just like them. I see both sides of this problem every day.

My North Star has always been impact. Helping one household at a time matters, and I'll never stop doing that. And training a generation of retirement specialists who each serve hundreds of households? That's how millions of retirees get the guidance they need.

But none of that matters if you don't know how to find the right expertise. That's where you come in.

Whether you're within five years of retirement or already living it, whether you're working with an advisor or considering a change, this book gives you the tools to make better decisions about one of the most important professional relationships of your life.

It gives you a framework for evaluating advisors without relying on marketing language or fancy titles. It helps you avoid becoming an accidental experiment while someone else learns retirement income planning with your life savings.

You earned this money over decades of work. You deserve advice that matches the complexity of the next phase of your life.

Retirement isn't the finish line. It's a new chapter. And it requires a different kind of guide.

That specialist exists.

And by the time you finish this book, you'll know how to find them. Let's begin.

# Chapter 1: You Don't Ask Your Family Doctor to Perform Heart Surgery

*"Never ask a barber if you need a haircut."*

— Warren Buffett

Sarah and Tom walked into my office with a problem they didn't know they had.

They were 64 and 62, with $2.3 million in retirement savings. Sarah was planning to retire within the year. Tom had already left his corporate job. They'd worked with the same financial advisor for nineteen years, someone who had helped them build substantial wealth. By all appearances, they were set.

"Our advisor says we're fine," Sarah told me. "He showed us an analysis that shows we have an 89% probability of success. To be honest, I don't really know what that means. Is that like getting a 'B'? Either way, something feels off. We don't actually have a plan for how to live on this money. Just a projection that says it should work out."

I asked to see their retirement income plan.

They handed me a single page showing portfolio projections under different return scenarios.

I asked about their Social Security strategy. Tom had already claimed at 62. His full retirement age was 66. Sarah was planning to claim at 64.

"Did your advisor analyze different claiming strategies?" I asked.

"He said to claim whenever we thought we wanted the money," Sarah said.

I asked about their tax situation. Both had substantial pre-tax 401(k) balances. Required minimum distributions would begin at age 73, forcing large taxable withdrawals whether they needed the money or not.

"Has your advisor discussed Roth conversions? You have a five-year window before RMDs where your income is lower. That's usually prime time to move money from pre-tax to Roth at favorable rates."

Sarah looked at Tom. "What's a Roth conversion?"

I asked how they planned to take withdrawals. Which accounts first? In what order?

"He said to take a little from each account proportionally, to keep our allocation balanced."

That's when I realized: they didn't have a retirement income plan. They had a portfolio. And their advisor, despite being competent and well-intentioned, had no idea how to turn that portfolio into a sustainable retirement income strategy.

He'd never been trained to.

Over the next three months, we built what they should have had all along:

A Social Security claiming strategy that, even though Tom had already claimed sub-optimally, would add $89,000 in lifetime benefits by having Sarah delay to age 70.

A five-year Roth conversion plan would save an estimated $175,000 in taxes over their retirement.

A tax-efficient withdrawal sequence that specified which accounts to tap when, coordinated with their tax brackets and RMD timeline.

A systematic approach to managing withdrawals during market volatility, with cash reserves and rules for when to stop portfolio distributions during downturns.

The cost of their advisor's knowledge gap? Over $250,000 in missed opportunities, just in the areas we could quantify.

And here's the thing: their advisor wasn't incompetent. He wasn't unethical. He wasn't lazy.

He was a generalist advisor trying to do a retirement income specialist's job.

## When I Realized Financial Planning Needed Specialists

That meeting with Sarah and Tom reminded me of something from my first career.

Before I became a financial advisor, I was an airline pilot. I'd landed the job after 9/11 turned the aviation industry upside down, and I spent years flying commercial aircraft. I had thousands of hours in simulators, rigorous training, and a commercial pilot's license.

But you know what I couldn't do?

Fly a fighter jet in combat. Land a helicopter on an aircraft carrier. Test a new experimental aircraft. Pilot a rescue helicopter in mountainous terrain.

Why? Because different aircraft require different skills. Different missions require different training. A commercial pilot is trained for smooth, safe, predictable passenger transport. A fighter pilot is trained for high-G maneuvers and combat scenarios. A helicopter pilot masters entirely different physics and handling characteristics.

Nobody questions this. You wouldn't want me flying an F-16 just because I could fly a 737. The foundational knowledge overlaps, sure. We all understand aerodynamics, navigation, and flight instruments. But the specialized expertise is entirely different.

I left aviation to pursue my real passion, helping people with their finances. I'd grown up talking about the Wall Street Journal at the dinner table with my dad, who was a CFO, and I loved the intersection of numbers, planning, and genuinely helping people. Financial planning seemed like the perfect career.

My timing, as it turned out, was spectacularly terrible. Eighteen months after I started as a financial advisor, the market crashed nearly 50% during the Great Recession.

But that experience taught me something invaluable: financial planning isn't one job. It's several different jobs, requiring different expertise, at different life stages.

Yet in financial services, we routinely expect advisors trained in wealth accumulation to handle retirement income distribution. As if they're the same job.

They're not.

## Why Specialization Exists

Think about the last time you needed professional help for something serious.

If you needed heart surgery, you didn't ask your family doctor to perform it. You went to a cardiologist, probably a cardiothoracic surgeon who has performed hundreds of these procedures.

If you were sued, you didn't hire a real estate attorney to defend you in court. You found a litigator who specializes in that type of case.

If your roof was leaking, you didn't call a general contractor and hope they knew roofing. You called a roofing specialist.

This pattern exists everywhere in professional services:

Medicine has dozens of specialties. Your primary care physician manages your overall health, but refers you to an oncologist for cancer, an orthopedic surgeon for joint problems, a dermatologist for skin issues, a neurologist for brain conditions.

Law has criminal defense, corporate law, tax law, estate planning, intellectual property, family law. An attorney who excels at negotiating business contracts isn't qualified to defend you in a murder trial.

Engineering has civil, mechanical, electrical, chemical, and aerospace subspecialties. You don't hire a chemical engineer to design a bridge.

Architecture has residential, commercial, industrial, and landscape specializations. Different projects require different expertise.

The pattern is universal: as fields mature and knowledge deepens, specialization emerges. It's not because generalists are bad at their jobs. It's because the body of knowledge in any given area becomes too vast for one person to master everything.

Medicine recognized this a century ago. You wouldn't want a doctor trained in the 1920s practicing general medicine today to perform your modern bypass surgery using techniques developed in the 1980s and refined over the past forty years.

Yet the financial services industry is about fifty years behind.

## The Two Different Jobs: Wealth Accumulation vs. Retirement Income

Let me be specific about what makes these phases so fundamentally different.

### Wealth Accumulation: Building Wealth

During your working years, financial planning has a clear objective: maximize growth while managing risk appropriate to your time horizon.

You're adding money regularly through paychecks and contributions. Market crashes, while unpleasant, aren't catastrophic because you're not withdrawing anything. In fact, downturns are opportunities to buy more shares at lower prices. You have time to recover.

Your advisor's job during the growth phase includes:

- Asset allocation based on your risk tolerance and time horizon
- Portfolio diversification across asset classes
- Tax-deferred saving strategies (maximizing 401(k) and IRA contributions)
- Rebalancing to maintain target allocations
- Helping you stay disciplined and not panic-sell during volatility
- Monitoring performance relative to appropriate benchmarks

The goal is growth. The time horizon is long, twenty to forty years. The math is straightforward: contribute consistently, earn reasonable returns, let compounding work in your favor.

Volatility is manageable because you're not taking withdrawals. You're adding money during downturns, which actually smooths out your average cost per share.

These are the skills most financial advisors are trained in. This is what the Certified Financial Planner (CFP®) designation largely focuses on. This is the culture of many large firms. This is wealth accumulation planning.

More precisely, they do help people create plans *to get to* retirement, not for life *in* retirement.

**Decumulation: Sustainable Income**

Retirement flips everything.

Now you're withdrawing money instead of adding it. Instead of decades to recover from losses, you might need that money next year for living expenses. Instead of one goal (growth), you have competing priorities: generating income, managing taxes, preserving capital, leaving a legacy, ensuring your money lasts as long as you do.

Most critically, you face risks during decumulation that simply didn't matter during your wealth-building years:

**Sequence of returns risk:** It's not just about average returns over your retirement. It's about when those returns happen. If you experience major market losses early in retirement while taking withdrawals, you can permanently damage your portfolio's sustainability. You're selling shares at depressed prices to generate income, which means you have fewer shares to participate in the eventual recovery.

This is what happened to so many people who retired in 2007-2008. Their portfolios dropped 40-50%, and they were taking withdrawals to live on. Even after the market recovered, their portfolios never fully caught up because they'd sold shares at the bottom.

**Longevity risk:** You might live to 95. Your spouse might live to 100. How does your plan account for forty years of retirement? Inflation alone will cut your purchasing power in half. Healthcare costs will increase. Long-term care might be needed. Your advisor needs to plan not just for the next five years, but for the next three decades.

**Tax complexity:** During wealth accumulation, tax planning advice usually means: defer, defer, defer. Max out your 401(k), contribute to IRAs, and delay taxation as long as possible. The problem with that advice is that you end up with a ticking time bomb of taxes when it's time to take money out.

In retirement, the calculus changes completely. You now have multiple "buckets" of money taxed differently: pre-tax retirement accounts, Roth accounts, and taxable investment accounts. The order in which you withdraw from these accounts can make a six-figure difference over your retirement.

Plus, you have required minimum distributions looming at age 73, a portion of your Social Security benefits that will be taxable depending on your income, Medicare premiums that increase with income, and Roth conversion opportunities that need to be considered.

This isn't "file your taxes, and you're done." This is multi-year strategic tax planning requiring sophisticated analysis.

**Withdrawal strategy complexity:** How much can you safely withdraw? The old "4% rule" is a very rough starting point, not a plan. Should you spend more in early retirement when you're active and less later? How do you adjust withdrawals during market downturns? When do you tap different accounts? How do you coordinate Social Security timing, pension decisions (if applicable), portfolio withdrawals, and perhaps part-time work income?

These are not questions your wealth-building advisor was trained to answer.

Your advisor's job during decumulation includes everything from wealth building, PLUS:

- Creating sustainable withdrawal strategies customized to your specific situation
- Tax-efficient distribution sequencing across multiple account types
- Social Security claiming optimization (often worth $100,000+ in lifetime benefits)
- Medicare navigation and healthcare cost planning
- Long-term care funding strategies
- Managing sequence of returns risk through bucketing, floor-income strategies, or systematic withdrawal policies
- Estate and legacy planning integrated with income needs
- Ongoing monitoring and adjustment as circumstances change

This is specialized knowledge. This is what the Retirement Income Certified Professional (RICP®) program I direct consists of: three intensive courses, eighteen specialized domains of retirement income expertise, hundreds of hours of study.

Most advisors have never taken a single course dedicated exclusively to retirement income planning.

## Why the Skills Don't Transfer

"But my advisor is smart and experienced," you might be thinking. "They've managed my money for twenty years. Surely they can figure this out."

Maybe. But do you want them learning on the job with your money when you're in your sixties and seventies, when mistakes are catastrophic and time to recover is limited?

Being a good accumulation advisor doesn't make you a bad person. It just doesn't automatically make you qualified for retirement income planning.

It's like being an excellent general practice attorney doesn't qualify you to argue appellate cases. The foundational knowledge overlaps, but the specialized expertise is different.

Consider what happens when an accumulation-trained advisor encounters retirement income without proper training:

**They apply accumulation strategies to a decumulation problem.** They keep your portfolio allocation the same as when you were 50 because "that worked." They continue measuring success against benchmarks (how'd we do versus the S&P 500?) rather than measuring income sustainability. They tell you to "stay the course" during downturns without having a systematic policy for adjusting withdrawals.

**They keep measuring success by portfolio performance.** But in retirement, beating the market matters less than sustainable income that lasts a lifetime. A portfolio that grows 12% one year but forces you to sell 30% down the next year during a crash isn't successful, it's dangerous.

**They miss massive opportunities.** The years between retirement and age 73 (when required minimum distributions begin) are often ideal for Roth conversions, strategically moving money from pre-tax accounts to Roth at lower tax rates. This can save enormous amounts in taxes over retirement. Most accumulation advisors never bring it up because they're not thinking proactively about multi-year tax strategy.

**They don't recognize retirement-specific risks.** Sequence of returns risk isn't relevant during accumulation, so many advisors don't understand it. They've never built a withdrawal policy statement. They've never stress-tested a portfolio for sustainable withdrawals over thirty years, which is an entirely different calculation than projecting growth.

## The Stakes Are Higher in Retirement

Here's the key difference that needs to be said clearly:

In retirement, you might never earn back your losses.

During your working years, if the market crashed and your portfolio dropped 30%, it was painful but recoverable. You kept contributing from your paycheck. You bought shares at lower prices. You had time. A market crash in your forties or fifties was a setback, not a disaster.

In retirement, a market crash while you're taking withdrawals is different. If your portfolio drops 30% and you're withdrawing 5% annually to live on, you're selling shares at depressed prices just to generate income. Those shares can't recover because you've sold them. They're gone.

The remaining portfolio has to generate all your future income from a smaller base.

This is why sequence of returns risk is so devastating. This is why your retirement income plan needs strategies for managing this risk: cash reserves, withdrawal policy statements, dynamic spending rules, and bucketing strategies.

This is why the "stay the course" advice that worked beautifully during accumulation can be catastrophic during retirement.

And this is why people hire a retirement income specialist.

## Moving On

You understand the distinction now. Accumulation and decumulation require different expertise, different strategies, different risk management.

But here's the question most people ask at this point: if this difference is so fundamental, why isn't every financial advisor trained in retirement income planning? Why is specialized expertise the exception rather than the rule?

The answer lies in how retirement itself has changed over the past 50 years, and how the financial services industry has struggled to keep pace.

That's what we'll explore next.

## Three Key Takeaways:

- **Accumulation and decumulation require fundamentally different expertise.** During your working years, market volatility is manageable because you're adding money and have time to recover. In retirement, withdrawing during market downturns creates sequence of returns risk: selling shares at depressed prices permanently damages your portfolio's ability to generate future income.

- **Success at wealth building doesn't automatically transfer to retirement income planning.** An advisor who helped you accumulate $2 million may have no specialized training in tax-efficient withdrawal sequencing, Social Security optimization, or managing sustainable distributions across 30+ years. These require different knowledge than portfolio construction and asset allocation.

- **You need a specialist, not a generalist applying accumulation strategies.** Just as you wouldn't ask your family doctor to perform heart surgery, you shouldn't expect an accumulation-focused advisor to have retirement income expertise without specialized training. The stakes are too high. You may never earn back losses when you're taking withdrawals to live on.

# Chapter 2: The Emergence of Retirement Income as a Distinct Specialty

*"Change is the law of life. And those who look only to the past or present are certain to miss the future."*

— John F. Kennedy

In the mid-1970s, my grandfather on my dad's side stopped working for good. He'd spent his life doing physical labor, taking whatever jobs he could after returning from WWII: delivering ice, hauling coal, assembling furniture at a woodworking company. By his mid-sixties, his body was worn down from decades of hard work and recurring health issues from the war.

He had no retirement savings. None. He didn't believe in investing in stocks because his own parents had lost everything in the Great Depression. For him, the stock market was gambling, pure and simple. He lived on a small Social Security check and even smaller pension as a disabled veteran. He never had a company pension from any of his jobs. For the next twenty years, he barely left a ten-block radius of his house. Not because he was content staying close to home, but because he couldn't afford to go anywhere. He lived in borderline poverty.

My maternal grandfather didn't fare much better. He worked at a steel foundry his entire adult life and developed emphysema from the conditions. The company went bankrupt around the time he retired, and his pension vanished with it. Decades of loyalty, and nothing to show for it. He worked until he died, selling vegetables from his garden to local restaurants and running a small carpet-cleaning business. Not because he loved working, but because he had no choice.

These weren't lazy men. They weren't poor planners. They simply lived in an era when retirement, as we understand it today, barely existed for working-class Americans. You worked until your body gave out, lived on whatever Social Security provided, and hoped your kids would help if things got bad.

Watching my grandfather's experiences is one of the main reasons I went into this profession. I didn't want other families to experience the kind of retirements they did, where financial stress overshadowed what should have been years of rest and dignity.

But here's what's striking: retirement today looks completely different than it did for my grandfathers, yet many financial advisors serving retirees are still using approaches designed for a world that no longer exists.

## The New Retirement Reality

Recently, I met with a woman who just retired from a manufacturing company, not unlike where my grandfathers worked. She's 63 years old. But her retirement has no resemblance to theirs.

She has $1.3 million in her 401(k), accumulated over 30 years of consistent contributions and company matches, plus $600,000 in a brokerage account. No pension. Social Security will cover about 28% of her income needs. She'll need to buy health insurance until Medicare kicks in at 65, costing roughly $1,500 per month. No retiree health benefits from her employer.

My job as her advisor? Make that $1.9 million generate reliable income for potentially 30 years or more, while managing taxes across multiple account types, optimizing Social Security timing, navigating Medicare, adapting her portfolio to the every-changing economy, and ensuring the money lasts whether she lives to 85 or 105.

The problem has completely flipped. My grandfathers had too little money and no real plan. Today's retirees often have substantial savings but face the complex challenge of making it last three decades.

That's why retirement income planning emerged as a distinct specialty. Not because advisors wanted another designation to hang on the wall, but because the fundamental nature of retirement changed, and with it, the expertise required to navigate it successfully.

And it happened over just two generations.

## How We Got Here: A Century of Retirement Evolution

To understand why retirement income planning emerged as a distinct specialty, you need to understand how radically retirement itself has changed.

### 1935-1950: Retirement Barely Exists

When Social Security was created in 1935, the retirement age was set at 65. At the time, average life expectancy was 61. The program was designed to support the small percentage of people who lived past working age for a few years.

Just how small? Less than 3% of the population was 65 or older in 1850. It was only 7% by 1940. Retirement wasn't a life stage most people experienced.

And for those who did reach retirement age, they typically kept working anyway. In 1880, more than three-quarters of men older than 64 were still in the labor force. Eighty-one percent of 70-year-olds were still working. Most people simply couldn't afford to stop.

For the small fraction who did retire, half lived with their children. There was no extended period of independent retirement living.

Consider this: if you were 20 years old in 1880, you could expect to spend less than 6% of your life in retirement, roughly 2.3 years. Compare that to someone who turned 20 in 1990, who can expect to spend up to one-third of their life in retirement.

That's the magnitude of change we're talking about. Retirement transformed from a brief, rare wind-down period into a multi-decade life stage spanning 20, 30, even 40 years.

Most people worked until they couldn't anymore, then relied on family support or modest Social Security benefits. "Retirement planning" wasn't really a thing because retirement itself was brief and uncommon.

### 1950s-1970s: The Pension Era

After World War II, defined benefit pensions became standard for many corporate and government workers. You worked for a company for 20-30 years, retired with a pension that paid a percentage of your salary for life, added Social Security on top, and you were set.

Life expectancy increased to the mid-70s, so retirement expanded from a few years to 10-15 years. Still manageable with a pension.

Financial advisors during this era worked primarily with wealthy families who had accumulated substantial assets beyond their pensions, or were, for the most part, insurance salesmen. For most everyone else, the pension and Social Security handled retirement income. Any additional savings were just that: additional, not essential.

**1978-1990s: The 401(k) Revolution Begins**

In 1978, Congress passed a tax code revision that included Section 401(k), allowing employees to defer compensation into retirement accounts. Initially intended as a supplement to pensions, 401(k) plans quickly became the primary retirement vehicle as companies realized they could shift retirement risk from the company balance sheet to individual employees.

By the 1990s, new employees at many companies weren't offered pensions at all. Just a 401(k) with maybe a company match.

The shift was profound: instead of the company bearing investment risk, longevity risk, and inflation risk, employees now bore all of it.

But most people didn't realize what had changed. The prevailing assumption was to save in your 401(k), invest in mutual funds, accumulate wealth, and when you retire, just start withdrawing. How complicated could it be?

**1994: The First Research Breakthrough**

William Bengen, a financial planner, published an article in the *Journal of Financial Planning* that would change the conversation. He asked a deceptively simple question: "How much can retirees safely withdraw from their portfolios without running out of money?"

Using historical market data from 1926 forward, he tested different withdrawal rates across various 30-year retirement periods. His conclusion: retirees could withdraw 4% of their portfolio in the first year, adjust for inflation each year thereafter, and have a high probability their money would last 30 years.

The "4% rule" was born.

More importantly, Bengen sparked something new: academics and practitioners began studying retirement income as its own domain, not just an extension of wealth building. To some extent, this happened because of advances in computing and access to historical market data.

Questions emerged that had never been systematically researched:

- What withdrawal strategies balance sustainability with spending flexibility?
- How should asset allocation change when you're taking distributions?
- What is the impact of negative returns early in retirement, and how do you manage it?
- How do you maximize Social Security benefits for spouses with different earning histories?

These weren't questions that mattered during the growth phase. They were retirement income-specific. And answering them required new knowledge.

**2000-2002: The First Wake-Up Call**

Then came the dot-com crash.

The S&P 500 dropped 9% in 2000, another 12% in 2001, and 22% in 2002. Three consecutive years of losses. People who retired in 1999 or 2000 watched their portfolios get hammered just as they started taking withdrawals. This was particularly difficult because this same cohort of investors had just experienced double-digit returns in the US stock market for the previous decade.

This was the first mass experience of sequence of returns risk for the 401(k) generation. Sequence risk is the danger that experiencing poor returns early in retirement can permanently damage your portfolio because you're forced to sell shares at depressed prices to generate income. Shares that might never recover because they're gone. Same average returns over 30 years, but devastating outcomes if the losses happen early when you're taking withdrawals.

For people still working and contributing to 401(k)s, the 2000-2002 crash was stressful but survivable. For retirees taking withdrawals, it was devastating.

The advice financial advisors had been giving, "stay the course, don't panic, time in the market beats timing the market," worked fine if you were 45 years old and still adding money. It was dangerous if you were 66 and withdrawing $50,000 annually.

Some advisors started to realize that we need different strategies for the distribution phase.

**2008-2009: The Second, More Memorable Wake-Up Call**

Just as portfolios recovered from the lost decade (10 years of 0% return), the financial crisis hit.

The market dropped nearly 50% from peak to trough. Retirees and near-retirees panicked. Many went to cash, locking in massive losses and missing the recovery.

I started my career as a financial advisor in September 2007, so I lived through this in real time. I watched sophisticated clients with significant portfolios, people who had worked with good advisors for years, make emotional decisions that permanently damaged their financial futures.

Why? Because their advisors had growth plans, not retirement income plans.

Their advisors told them to "stay the course" and "don't panic," which is generic advice that doesn't address the specific question retirees needed answered: "Can I still afford to retire? Should I cut my spending? By how much? For how long?"

Meanwhile, the small but growing number of advisors who had specialized in retirement income planning were doing something completely different for their clients.

They had withdrawal policy statements already in place that specified exactly what to do during severe downturns. They had 12-24 months of cash reserves set aside specifically so they could stop taking distributions from the stock portfolio and let it recover. They ran updated projections showing clients: "If we reduce discretionary spending by

15% for the next 18 months and tap our reserves, here's how the plan adjusts. We're still on track."

They'd already categorized their clients' spending into essential versus discretionary, so they knew exactly where adjustments could be made without threatening their lifestyle. They used the downturn to execute Roth conversions and tax-loss harvesting strategies. They revisited Social Security timing decisions, perhaps delaying claiming to preserve portfolio assets.

Most importantly, they had systematic frameworks for decision-making instead of leaving clients to make emotional choices in the moment.

The difference in outcomes was stark.

Fast forward to today, nearly two decades later. Clients who worked with retirement income specialists during that period generally navigated the crisis successfully. Their portfolios recovered. Their spending adjusted temporarily but returned to normal. They're enjoying the retirements they planned for.

Many clients who worked with growth-focused advisors? They're still dealing with the consequences of decisions made in panic during 2008-2009 or the market volatility during the spring of COVID-19. Portfolios that never fully recovered because they sold at the bottom. Permanently reduced spending because they didn't have a framework for temporary adjustments. Some had to delay retirement or return to work.

The 2008 crisis made the knowledge gap undeniable. Retirement income planning requires different expertise than wealth building. And most advisors didn't have it.

## Why Specialization Finally Emerged

Think about other professions and when specialization became normal.

I have a neighbor who is one of the top criminal defense attorneys in the State. When my wife and I needed estate planning documents drafted, did we use him? Of course not. We hired an estate planning *specialist*. Both lawyers who passed the bar exam, but the unknowing consumer might not realize how different their expertise is. Estate planning requires deep knowledge of tax law, trust structures, and wealth transfer strategies. Criminal defense requires mastery of criminal procedure, evidence rules, and trial advocacy.

In aviation, my first career, specialization is fundamental. I earned my commercial pilot license at age 20, but that didn't mean I could jump into any aircraft to carry passengers. Would you want a pilot who drops skydivers all day to suddenly fly you across the Atlantic in a 757? Same basic principles of flight, completely different aircraft systems, different procedures, different skills required.

In medicine, the shift to specialization happened about a century ago as medical knowledge exploded and it became impossible for one doctor to master everything. You wouldn't want your family doctor performing your heart surgery, no matter how much you trust them for annual checkups.

Financial services is following the same pattern, just later. For decades, the field was simple enough that one advisor could competently handle everything. But several forces converged to make specialization necessary:

**The complexity explosion.** Someone retiring today faces decisions about multiple account types with different tax treatments, Social Security claiming strategies, Medicare options, healthcare costs, long-term care funding, estate planning with constantly changing tax laws, withdrawal strategies that account for sequence risk, and tax optimization across 30+ years.

And here's what makes it even more challenging: the rules keep changing. The SECURE Act in 2019 changed required minimum distribution ages from 70½ to 72. SECURE 2.0 in 2022 changed it again to 73, and it will move to 75 in 2033. It also changed rules around Roth conversions, 401(k) catch-up contributions, and qualified charitable distributions, just to name a few.

Then came the OBBBA Act with more modifications. Each piece of legislation provides benefits to consumers, but also adds layers of complexity. An advisor who learned retirement planning rules ten years ago needs continuous education just to stay current on what's changed, let alone master the deeper strategies.

This is sophisticated, specialized work that requires staying current with evolving research and constantly changing regulations.

**The risk transfer**. When pensions handled most retirement income, advisors managed supplemental assets. Now they're managing the primary income source. The stakes are completely different.

**The research base.** We now have decades of academic research on retirement income strategies, withdrawal rates, tax optimization, Social Security timing, and behavioral finance in retirement. This body of knowledge didn't exist 30 years ago.

**Longer retirements**. A 65-year-old today might live to 95. Planning for a 30-year retirement is fundamentally different than planning for a 10-year retirement.

All of this meant that general financial planning training, while valuable, wasn't sufficient for specialized retirement income work.

## The Professionalization of Expertise

As the need became clear, specialized training emerged.

The American College of Financial Services, where I direct the Center for Retirement Income, launched the Retirement Income Certified Professional (RICP®) designation in 2012. This was the first comprehensive credential focused exclusively on retirement income planning.

The curriculum consists of three intensive courses covering retirement income processes, income sources, tax strategies, Social Security optimization, healthcare planning, and ongoing plan management. It requires several months of intense study, proctored exams, three years of experience, and annual continuing education.

Other organizations developed their own retirement income training programs. Universities began offering specialized courses. Conferences dedicated entirely to retirement income research and best practices emerged.

The point isn't that RICP® is the only path to expertise. It's that retirement income planning became recognized as a specialty requiring dedicated training, just like other professional specializations.

Consider the difference in depth between general and specialized training.

The CFP® certification, which I hold and deeply value, covers retirement planning as one component among many:

investments, insurance, tax, estate planning. In most CFP® education programs, retirement income topics represent just 11% of the curriculum!

Specialized retirement income training devotes 100% of its focus to this one phase of financial life. That's the difference between a general practitioner's knowledge of cardiology and a cardiologist's expertise.

Both are valuable. Both are needed. But they serve different purposes. CFP® provides broad competency across all financial planning areas. Specialized retirement income training provides deep expertise in this specific, complex domain.

## What This Means in Practice

When I work with a client at Stockbridge Private Wealth Management (www.stockbridgewealth.com), the analysis we conduct goes far beyond what general financial planning typically covers.

We're modeling Social Security claiming strategies, analyzing whether claiming at 62, full retirement age, or 70 makes sense given their health, family longevity, other income sources, and tax situation. We're running scenarios showing the lifetime benefit difference of various strategies, often $100,000 or more.

We're creating multi-year tax projections, identifying opportunities for Roth conversions in low-income years before required minimum distributions begin at 73. We're modeling how different withdrawal sequences affect their tax brackets over the next 20 years.

We're building withdrawal strategies that specify which accounts to tap in which order, how to adjust during market downturns, when to use cash reserves versus continuing portfolio distributions. We're creating written policy statements so there's a systematic framework for decisions, not emotional reactions.

We're analyzing Medicare options, modeling healthcare costs with inflation, and evaluating long-term care funding strategies. We're coordinating with CPAs and estate attorneys to ensure the financial plan integrates with tax and legal planning.

This level of analysis requires specialized knowledge that most advisors simply haven't studied.

## The Evidence-Based Shift

Another significant development has been the move toward evidence-based retirement income strategies.

During the growth phase, evidence-based investing meant low-cost, diversified portfolios instead of trying to pick winning stocks or time markets. This was supported by decades of research showing that markets are largely efficient, active management rarely beats benchmarks after fees, and asset allocation drives most returns.

That same research rigor now applies to retirement income. Studies examine which withdrawal strategies optimize spending while maintaining sustainability, how asset allocation should evolve through retirement, the optimal sequence for tapping different account types, and how much Social Security timing really matters.

At my firm, we've built our practice around evidence-based approaches. We focus on controllable factors: minimizing costs through low-cost ETFs, optimizing taxes through strategic withdrawal sequencing, managing risk through asset allocation rather than stock picking, maintaining discipline through systematic frameworks.

Different advisors with specialized training might reach different strategic conclusions based on the same research. That's fine. What matters is that decisions are grounded in evidence and analysis, not product sales incentives, proprietary investment strategies, or so called "rules-of-thumb".

## The Reality Check

Here's what I've learned over 20 years: retirement income planning isn't financial planning with minor adjustments. It's a fundamentally different discipline.

- The questions are different.
- The risks are different.
- The strategies are different.
- The stakes are higher.
- The time to recover from mistakes is shorter.

That requires specialized expertise.

The good news? That expertise exists now. The research base exists. The training programs exist. Specialists who have dedicated their careers to this specific phase of financial life exist.

The question isn't whether you can find qualified retirement income specialists. The question is whether you're currently working with one.

And that brings us to the hardest part of this realization: what happens when you've worked with an advisor for 15 or 20 years, you like them, you're grateful they helped you build wealth, but you're starting to recognize they may not have the specialized training required for the next phase?

How do you handle the moment when loyalty and competence come into conflict?

That's what we'll tackle in the next chapter.

## Three Key Takeaways:

- **Modern retirement is fundamentally different from previous generations.** The shift from pensions to 401(k)s transferred all investment, longevity, and inflation risk from companies to individuals. Combined with 30-40 year retirements instead of 10-15 years, this created planning challenges that simply didn't exist when pensions provided guaranteed income for life.

- **The 2000-2002 and 2008-2009 market crashes revealed the knowledge gap.** These crises showed that "stay the course" advice works during accumulation but can be devastating during retirement. Advisors with specialized retirement income training had systematic frameworks, withdrawal policy statements, cash reserves, spending guardrails that protected clients. Generalists didn't, and their clients often made emotional decisions that permanently damaged their financial futures.

- **Retirement income planning became a recognized academic discipline requiring specialized training.** Beginning with William Bengen's 4% rule research in 1994, decades of study created a specialized body of knowledge covering withdrawal strategies, sequence of returns risk, tax optimization, and Social Security claiming. The RICP® designation emerged in 2012 as the first comprehensive credential focused exclusively on this specialty, representing 100% depth on retirement income versus the 11% coverage in general CFP® training.

# Chapter 3: When Loyalty Becomes a Liability

*"Loyalty to petrified opinion never yet broke a chain or freed a human soul."*

— Mark Twain

Let me tell you about a conversation I had with a prospective client a few years ago. We'll call her Margaret.

Margaret was 63, recently retired from a career in healthcare administration, and had about $2.1 million in retirement assets. She'd been working with her financial advisor, Steve, for nearly 20 years. Steve had helped her through a divorce in her mid-forties, guided her through market volatility, encouraged her to keep contributing to her 401(k) even when it was tempting not to, and genuinely celebrated with her when she hit her retirement savings goals.

"Steve is a wonderful person," Margaret told me in our first meeting. "He's been there through everything. I trust him completely."

"So why are you here?" I asked.

She hesitated. "I feel terrible even talking to you. Like I'm betraying him. But I'm worried about something specific."

She pulled out a document from her bag. "This is what Steve gave me as my 'retirement income plan.'"

I looked at it. One page. It showed:

Income replacement goal: 80% of pre-retirement income

Withdrawal rate: 4% annually

Social Security: Starting at age 65

Spending: Increased by 3% each year for inflation

Result: Monte Carlo simulation showing "78% probability of success."

"What about the rest of the plan?" I asked.

"That's it," she said. "When I asked him what the 78% probability of success meant, he said it means there's a 78% chance my money lasts my lifetime based on historical market returns. Which I guess is good? But it also means there's a 22% chance I run out of money, and that seems terrifying."

She paused. "And when I started asking more detailed questions, like *'Should I actually claim Social Security at 65? Is 4% the right amount for me specifically? What accounts should I withdraw from first? Should we be doing anything with Roth conversions?'* he kind of brushed them off. He said the Monte Carlo accounts for all of that, and 78% is a passing grade."

Margaret looked uncomfortable. "I started doing some reading on my own. Retirement income planning blogs, some books. And I realized Steve never analyzed different Social Security claiming ages for me. He just assumed 65. He never talked about which accounts to tap first for tax efficiency. He never mentioned Roth conversions at all. The 4% withdrawal and 80% replacement ratio, those aren't based on *my* situation. They're just generic industry assumptions!"

She shook her head. "Steve has been wonderful for 20 years. He helped me save aggressively after my divorce. He kept me from panic-selling in 2008. He's a genuinely good person who cares about me, and we even go to the same church. But I don't think he actually knows how to create a retirement income plan. And I feel terrible for even thinking that, let alone sitting here talking to you about it."

## The "They Got Me Here" Fallacy

There's a powerful emotional logic that keeps people with advisors even when those advisors aren't qualified for the current phase of their financial life. It goes something like this:

"My advisor helped me build this wealth. They gave me good advice. They kept me disciplined. They helped me set up a 529 for my kids. I wouldn't be in this position without them. Therefore, they must be the right person to help me manage this wealth in retirement."

Can you spot the flaw in this reasoning?

The conclusion doesn't follow from the premises. Being excellent at accumulation planning and being excellent at retirement income planning are two different skill sets. Someone can be outstanding at the first and entirely unqualified for the second.

Think about other areas of life where we understand this instinctively. The contractor who built your house might be wonderful at new construction but completely wrong for a historic restoration. The attorney who handled your real estate closing probably shouldn't defend you in a criminal trial. The coach who developed your tennis serve isn't the right person to rehab your torn rotator cuff.

In each case, you're grateful for what that professional did for you in their area of expertise. But you recognize that a new challenge requires different expertise, even if that means working with someone new.

Yet when it comes to financial advisors, we struggle with this distinction. Why?

Part of it is the personal relationship. Money is deeply emotional. You've likely shared your fears, hopes, and life circumstances with your advisor. They know your family. They've been through ups and downs with you. That creates a bond that feels like it would be disloyal to break.

Part of it is the success you've achieved together. Your advisor's strategies worked. You reached your goals. Why would you leave someone who has a proven track record with you?

And part of it is practical uncertainty. Even if you recognize your current advisor lacks specialized retirement income training, what's the alternative? How do you even find a retirement income specialist? And won't they just try to sell you an annuity or push you into dividend stocks? At least you know what you have with your current advisor, even if it's not perfect.

These are all understandable feelings. They're also, potentially, very expensive feelings.

## What Loyalty Actually Costs

Let me be specific about what staying with an unqualified advisor might cost you.

It's not just about dollar amounts, though those matter. It's about whether you can actually retire when you want to. Whether you can afford the retirement lifestyle you've been working toward for 30 years. Whether you'll spend your retirement years confident and relaxed, or anxious and second-guessing every expense.

I've seen clients discover, after working with a retirement income specialist, that better planning would have allowed them to retire two or three years earlier than they thought possible. Others realize they've been spending less than they could safely afford because their advisor gave them overly conservative guidance without any systematic analysis.

Some find out they're taking more risk than necessary because their advisor never built proper withdrawal strategies - they're spending at levels that might work in good markets but could force drastic cuts if we hit another 2008-style downturn in their first few years of retirement.

The decisions you make in the first five to ten years of retirement around Social Security timing, tax planning, and withdrawal strategies don't just affect your account balance. They affect whether you can afford that European trip you've been planning. Whether you need to delay retirement. Whether you're constantly worried about money or confident in your plan.

Suboptimal planning doesn't just cost you money. It costs you the retirement you've been working toward.

So while loyalty is admirable, it can also be expensive in ways that really matter. The question isn't whether you should be grateful for past help. The question is whether gratitude obligates you to continue with someone who may not be qualified to help you achieve the retirement you want.

I'd argue it doesn't.

## Why Good Advisors Don't Always Recognize Their Gaps

Here's something that makes this situation even more complicated: many advisors who lack retirement income expertise don't realize they lack it.

This isn't dishonesty or malice. It's a well-documented psychological phenomenon. When you don't know what you don't know, you're not equipped to recognize the gaps in your knowledge. You genuinely believe you're competent because you're unaware of all the things you've never learned.

Think about your own areas of expertise. If you've spent 30 years in healthcare, you know the depths of medical knowledge you possess and all the specialized training you've undertaken. If someone with two years of college biology classes tried to give medical advice, you'd instantly recognize how much they were missing.

But that person might not recognize it themselves. They've read some articles. They understand basic concepts. They might even give advice that sounds reasonable to a layperson. They don't have the training to understand how much more depth exists beyond their surface-level knowledge.

The same thing happens in financial services. An advisor who has spent 20 years helping clients accumulate wealth knows a lot about portfolio construction, asset allocation, and market behavior. They've been successful at what they do. They've helped many clients reach their goals.

But retirement income planning requires knowledge they may have never been exposed to. Detailed analysis of Social Security claiming strategies. Multi-year tax projection and Roth conversion optimization. Withdrawal sequencing across different account types. Strategies for managing the sequence of returns risk. Portfolio structuring specifically designed for systematic withdrawals rather than accumulation. Healthcare planning, including Medicare navigation and long-term care funding. Building withdrawal policy statements that provide systematic decision-making during volatile markets.

If they've never studied these topics in depth, they don't know how much there is to learn. So when a client asks about retirement planning, they apply their accumulation knowledge and assume it's sufficient. They're not trying to deceive anyone. They genuinely believe they're equipped for the task.

This is one reason why the question "How long have you been a financial advisor?" isn't particularly useful when evaluating retirement income expertise. An advisor with 25 years of experience might have 25 years of accumulation planning experience and zero years of specialized retirement income training. For example, one of my financial planner friends only works with people working in the tech sector and helps them analyze their stock options. When those same clients go to retire, she hands them off to a specialist. Her work is done.

What matters isn't how long they've been an advisor. What matters is whether they've invested in developing expertise specific to retirement income planning.

## The Conversation You're Avoiding

Let's return to Margaret for a moment.

After several meetings where we walked through comprehensive retirement income analysis, she decided to transfer her accounts to Stockbridge. But she was dreading the conversation with Steve, her long-time advisor.

"What do I say?" she asked me. "I don't want to hurt his feelings. He's been so good to me."

I gave her a simple script:

"Steve, I've really appreciated your guidance over the past 20 years. You've helped me reach my retirement goals, and I'm grateful for that. As I've transitioned into retirement, I've realized I need specialized expertise in retirement income planning, specifically around managing withdrawals, tax strategy, Social Security optimization, and portfolio structuring for distributions rather than growth. I've decided to work with an advisor who focuses exclusively on this area. I wanted to let you know directly and thank you for everything you've done."

She used that script. And here's what happened: Steve was *not* disappointed. He understood. He acknowledged that several of his clients were reaching retirement age and that the planning needs were different than what he'd focused on throughout his career. He wished her well and helped facilitate a smooth transition.

That's how a professional advisor responds. No guilt trips. No defensiveness. No claims that specialized training doesn't matter. Just an acknowledgment that different phases of financial life require different expertise, and sometimes that means clients need to find specialists.

Not every advisor responds this way, and that itself is informative. An advisor who gets defensive when you mention seeking specialized expertise, who minimizes the importance of retirement income-specific knowledge, who suggests you're being disloyal, or who can't articulate what specific strategies they would implement for managing your portfolio during the withdrawal phase is telling you something important about their professionalism and their actual competence.

## The Consolidation Reality

I want to share a different story because it illustrates another common situation I see.

A couple, Tom and Linda, came to see me when Tom was 59 and starting to think seriously about early retirement at 62.

"Here's our situation," Tom said, pulling out a stack of statements. "We've got accounts all over the place. I have a 401(k) at my current employer and two old 401(k)s from previous jobs. Linda has her 403(b) and a rollover IRA. We have a joint taxable account at one brokerage, some individual accounts at another, and our old advisor from 15 years ago still manages about $300,000 for us that we kind of forgot about."

"Who's coordinating all of this?" I asked.

"That's the problem," Linda said. "Nobody is. We've got three different advisors looking at pieces of it, but nobody looking at the whole picture. And now that we're getting close to retirement, I'm realizing that's going to be a disaster. When Tom turns 73 and has to take required minimum distributions from three different accounts, who's going to figure out the tax-efficient way to do that? When we need to start doing Roth conversions, which advisor is going to coordinate across all these accounts?"

She looked frustrated. "You know what I realized? We have one dentist. One primary care doctor. But we have three financial advisors, and none of them are talking to each other. It's ridiculous."

I spent several meetings with them, doing exactly what Linda described: looking at everything together. We analyzed all their accounts, ran comprehensive retirement income projections, identified which accounts should be consolidated and which should be rolled over, mapped out a multi-year Roth conversion strategy that would require coordinating withdrawals across multiple account types, and built a Social Security claiming strategy that integrated with their overall income plan.

"This is the first time anyone has looked at our complete financial picture," Tom said. "Every other advisor just wanted to manage the money we gave them. Nobody wanted to think about how it all fits together for retirement."

They moved everything to Stockbridge. Not because their previous advisors were incompetent, but because they needed one person looking at the complete picture and implementing a coordinated strategy.

This happens more often than you might think. During accumulation, having accounts scattered across different places isn't a huge problem. You're just trying to save and invest. But in retirement, when you need tax-efficient withdrawal sequencing, coordinated RMD planning, strategic Roth conversions, and systematic portfolio management across all your assets, fragmentation becomes expensive.

I like to ask prospective clients: "Do you have two dentists? One for the left side of your mouth and one for the right?"

They laugh. "Of course not."

"So why do you have three financial advisors, none of whom are coordinating with each other?"

The goal isn't to automatically consolidate everything with one advisor. But if you're approaching retirement and your financial life is fragmented across multiple advisors and institutions, you should seriously consider whether that structure makes sense for the next phase. Retirement income planning requires coordination. Someone needs to be looking at the whole picture.

Some people have one advisor who already does this. If that's you, great. Others discover they've accumulated advisors the way they've accumulated assets, piecemeal over the years, and nobody's quarterbacking the overall strategy. That's a problem you should solve before retirement, not during it.

## A Professional Decision, Not a Personal Betrayal

One of the most important mindset shifts I encourage clients to make is this: your relationship with your financial advisor is fundamentally a professional relationship, not a personal one.

Yes, money is emotional. Yes, you've likely shared personal information and built some degree of friendship. Yes, you should like and trust your advisor.

But ultimately, you're hiring someone to provide professional services. And when your needs change in ways that require different expertise, it's entirely appropriate to seek out that expertise, even if it means changing providers.

You wouldn't feel guilty about switching from a general contractor to a historic restoration specialist when renovating an old home. You wouldn't apologize for seeking a specialist surgeon instead of having your general practitioner attempt a complex procedure. You wouldn't stay with a divorce attorney when you need estate planning work done.

The same principle applies here. Accumulation planning and retirement income planning require different skill sets. If your advisor excels at the former but lacks training in the latter, seeking a specialist isn't betrayal. It's prudent.

This doesn't mean you need to burn bridges or make it contentious. The script I gave Margaret earlier is professional and respectful. It acknowledges the advisor's contributions while clearly stating that your needs have evolved in ways that require different expertise.

Most professional advisors will understand this. Those who don't understand it, or who try to make you feel guilty about it, are revealing something about their professionalism that's worth noting.

## The Path Forward

There's no single right answer for everyone. Some of you will realize your current advisor does have specialized retirement income expertise, and you should continue working with them. Some will discover your advisor lacks that training but is willing to collaborate with specialists or implement strategies you bring to them, which might be an acceptable path. Others will conclude you need to find a retirement income specialist.

What matters is that you make this decision based on a clear-eyed assessment of your advisor's qualifications and your needs, not based solely on loyalty to a past relationship.

Gratitude and competence are not the same thing. You can be genuinely thankful for what your advisor has done while recognizing that your needs have evolved beyond their area of expertise.

You're not betraying anyone by seeking specialized knowledge at a specialized time in your life. You're being responsible with your financial future.

Your next 30 years depend on having someone with deep expertise in the specialized areas of retirement income planning. If your current advisor has that expertise, wonderful. If they don't, loyalty shouldn't override your need for competence.

In the next chapter, we'll get specific about what that specialized knowledge actually looks like. I'm going to walk you through the technical domains that retirement income specialists need to master. This will help you evaluate whether your advisor has depth in these areas or whether they're applying surface-level knowledge to complex problems.

Because once you see how deep retirement income planning actually goes, you'll understand why specialization matters so much.

## Key Takeaways

- **The "they got me here" fallacy is expensive.** Success at accumulation planning doesn't automatically mean qualification for retirement income planning. Your advisor may have been excellent at helping you build wealth, but that different phase required different expertise than managing sustainable withdrawals for 30 years.
- **Good advisors often don't recognize their own knowledge gaps.** When you don't know what you don't know, you can't recognize missing expertise. Many advisors genuinely believe they're competent at retirement planning because they're unaware of specialized domains they've never studied.
- **Transitioning advisors is a professional decision, not a personal betrayal.** Your relationship with your financial advisor is ultimately a professional service engagement. When your needs change to require

different expertise, seeking specialized help is prudent, not disloyal. Professional advisors understand this and facilitate smooth transitions.

# Chapter 4: What Retirement Income Specialists Actually Do (And Why Investment Management is a Small Part)

*"In preparing for battle I have always found that plans are useless, but planning is indispensable."*

— Dwight D. Eisenhower

When David and Susan walked into my office at age 61, David had a straightforward request.

"I'm looking for someone to manage my investments in retirement," he said. "I've got $2.3 million across my 401(k), Roth IRA, and a taxable account. Pretty simple. My current advisor will probably keep managing my taxable account, and I'll start withdrawing 4% a year from my other accounts. What else should I be thinking about?"

I asked him a few questions.

"What about the company stock options that vest over the next two years as you transition out?

What are you planning to do with your deferred compensation?

Have you made a decision about your pension: lump sum or monthly annuity?

Do you know when you are planning to start Social Security?

How will you get health insurance from 62 to 65?

Should that $400,000 in your taxable account stay there, or should we reposition it before you retire to minimize future taxes?

When's the last time you updated your estate plan?

Have you thought about long-term care planning?

And by the way, where are you actually planning to live in retirement?"

David stared at me. "I thought those were all just... separate things. You know, legal stuff, HR benefits, personal decisions. I figured the financial advisor just manages the money."

That's when I realized: David, like most people approaching retirement, had no idea what comprehensive retirement income planning actually involves.

They didn't need an investment manager. Frankly, you can hire a robo-advisor for a low cost to do that. They needed someone who could help him answer the questions that really mattered:

- Can I afford the lifestyle I want?
- For how long?
- What could go wrong?
- If something goes wrong, what does plan B look like?
- How do I minimize taxes and maximize what I keep?
- And how do I make sure this gets simpler as I age, not more complicated?

These aren't investment questions. They're retirement income planning questions. And they require an entirely different skill set than managing a portfolio during the accumulation years.

## The Shift in Thinking: You Don't Need an "Investment Guy" Anymore

Here's the fundamental difference between what you needed during your working years and what you need now.

During accumulation, the primary question was: "How do I grow this money?"

Your advisor's job was relatively straightforward: build a diversified portfolio, keep you disciplined during market volatility, encourage you to contribute consistently, and generate reasonable returns over time. Success was measured in portfolio performance, account balances, and whether you were on track to hit your retirement savings goal.

In retirement, the questions change completely:

**"Can I afford my lifestyle without working?"**

It's not just "how'd my portfolio do last year?" but "can I travel twice a year, golf three times a week, buy a condo in Florida, and not worry about money for the next 30 years?"

**"How do I keep more of what I have?"** Tax planning becomes crucial because you're no longer deferring taxes. You're managing them across potentially 30 years of distributions, required minimum distributions, Social Security taxation, and Medicare premium surcharges.

**"What could go wrong, and how do I prevent it?"** The risks shift from "will my portfolio grow enough?" to "will I outlive my money? What if I need long-term care? What if markets crash early in my retirement? What if I become cognitively impaired and can't manage this myself?"

**"How does this get easier as I age, not harder?"** At 85, you won't want to be making complex financial decisions. How do we build a plan that simplifies over time?

Generalist advisors excel at answering the first question superficially (portfolio returns). Retirement income specialists address all four questions systematically.

Let me show you what that actually looks like in practice.

## Building Sustainable Income (Not Just Managing Investments)

Retirement income planning isn't about maximizing portfolio returns. It's about creating reliable cash flow that can support your lifestyle for potentially 30 or 40 years.

And I mean *your* lifestyle, not "the average retiree", whatever that means. This needs to be unique to you and your life.

This requires coordinating multiple income sources, each with different tax treatments, timing considerations, and strategic implications.

## Let me give you a real example of why this matters.

I worked with a couple who had about $5 million in investable assets. The husband had been a high-income earner throughout his career. His wife worked at an elementary school office. Before they started working with me, he'd already decided to claim his Social Security at 62 and invest it, thinking that would lead to more money over the long term.

It was a reasonable thought process. But it was based on analyzing only his own break-even age, the point at which delaying would pay off for him personally.

He passed away from an unusual cancer at 72.

His early claiming decision effectively locked his wife into a much lower survivor benefit for the rest of her life. If he'd delayed claiming until 70 (they certainly had the assets to do so), her survivor benefit would have been substantially higher, potentially $100,000 or more over her lifetime.

Fortunately, she has plenty of other assets and income. But many widows don't. And this is the critical mistake people make with Social Security: they think only about their own break-even age, not about the impact on their surviving spouse.

A retirement income specialist analyzes Social Security as part of the overall income plan, considering both spouses' longevity, the value of the survivor benefit, taxation of benefits, and how claiming timing affects the rest of the financial strategy.

**Portfolio withdrawals.** You'll likely need to generate income from your investment accounts. But which accounts do you tap first? In what sequence? How much do you withdraw in good markets versus bad markets? How do you coordinate withdrawals with your tax planning and other income sources?

This isn't "take 4% and hope for the best." It's a systematic strategy that adapts based on market conditions, tax brackets, and life circumstances.

**Pensions or deferred compensation**. If you're fortunate enough to have a pension, you face a critical decision: take the monthly annuity for life, or the lump sum? Many people don't realize this is a complex analysis involving your health, your spouse's situation, interest rate environments, the pension plan's financial stability, and how it fits into your overall income strategy.

If you have deferred compensation paying out over several years, that creates both opportunities and constraints for your tax planning and withdrawal strategy.

**Part-time work or business income.** Some retirees continue earning income, either through part-time work, consulting, or a small business. This affects your Social Security taxation, your Medicare premiums, and your overall withdrawal strategy. I had a client claim Social Security after he quit his main career, but he stayed at the company part-time. He didn't realize how his benefit was taxed and has regretted it ever since.

## Income sources many people don't know about:

**In-plan 401(k) income options.** Some 401(k) plans now offer the ability to annuitize a portion of your account, creating guaranteed lifetime income. Most growth-focused advisors don't even know to ask if your plan offers this option, let alone help you analyze whether it makes sense for your situation.

**Qualified Longevity Annuity Contracts** (QLACs). These allow you to use a portion of your IRA to purchase guaranteed income that starts at age 80 or 85, reducing your required minimum distributions in the meantime and creating an income floor for your later years when you might be less able to manage market volatility.

The coordination question: How do all these income sources work together to create the lifestyle you want? And how do they interact with your tax planning, healthcare costs, and risk management?

This is what retirement income planning looks like. Not investment management. Income orchestration across multiple sources, each with different characteristics and strategic implications.

## Keeping More: Tax Planning Across Three Decades

Most people think tax planning means filing their return each April. In retirement, it's a 30-year strategy that can make a six-figure difference in what you actually get to spend.

Here's the reality: during your working years, tax planning was simple. Maximize contributions to pre-tax retirement accounts. Defer, defer, defer. Your advisor might have helped you with tax-loss harvesting in taxable accounts, but that was about it.

In retirement, you're no longer deferring taxes. You're managing them. And the timeline looks like this:

**Ages 62-72:** For many retirees, these are low-income years. You've stopped working, Social Security might not have started yet or is just beginning, and required minimum distributions haven't kicked in. This is often the golden window for Roth conversions, where you are strategically moving money from pre-tax accounts to Roth accounts while you're in relatively low tax brackets.

**Age 65:** Medicare starts. Now you need to be aware of Income-Related Monthly Adjustment Amount (IRMAA) thresholds. If your income exceeds certain levels, your Medicare Part B and Part D premiums increase substantially. This affects how much you can convert to Roth, how much you withdraw from different accounts, and even whether you should realize capital gains in a given year.

**Age 70½:** Qualified Charitable Distributions (QCDs) become available. If you're charitably inclined, you can now direct up to $111,000 per year (as of 2026, indexed for inflation) from your IRA directly to charity. It satisfies your required minimum distribution but doesn't count as taxable income. For someone giving $10,000-$20,000 annually to charity, this is a huge tax benefit.

**Age 73**: Required minimum distributions begin. The IRS now forces you to take money out of your pre-tax retirement accounts whether you need it or not. If you haven't done strategic Roth conversions in your 60s and early 70s, you might find yourself pushed into high tax brackets by these mandatory distributions.

**Age 75+:** Depending on how much you've left in pre-tax accounts, your RMDs might be substantial. Combined with Social Security, pension income, and any portfolio withdrawals, you could be in higher tax brackets in your late 70s and 80s than you were while working.

## What does this look like in practice? Let me give you a real example.

I worked with a couple who retired in their early 60s with substantial retirement savings. Most of it was in pre-tax accounts, 401(k) rollovers, and traditional IRAs. They had some Roth money and some in taxable accounts, but the bulk was pre-tax.

We did about $250,000 worth of Roth conversions over several years. We were doing them annually in moderate amounts, but in 2020, when the market dropped sharply due to COVID, we did a larger conversion. Same thing in 2022 when stocks fell again.

Here's what made it work: we funded the tax payments from their short-term bond positions, but we allocated the converted Roth money to diversified stock ETFs. When the market recovered, the subsequent gains more than paid for the taxes on the conversions. The money in those Roth accounts has been growing tax-free ever since.

Years later, they decided to buy a house closer to family. We used money from their Roth accounts for a portion of the purchase, completely tax-free. No mortgage needed. No tax consequences. Just tax-free withdrawals to fund a major life goal.

Compare that to what would have happened without the strategic Roth conversions: they would have been forced to take large required minimum distributions starting at 73, pushing them into high tax brackets, increasing their Medicare premiums, and potentially forcing them to take even more out to pay the higher taxes. Over the course of retirement, we're talking about hundreds of thousands of dollars in tax savings.

This is what tax planning in retirement actually looks like. Not filing your return each year. Multi-year strategic projections, opportunistic conversions during market downturns, coordination with Medicare premium thresholds, charitable giving optimization, and withdrawal sequencing across different account types.

Growth-focused advisors don't typically do this because they've never been trained in it. They know how to manage portfolios. Tax planning at this level is a different skill set entirely.

## Managing What Could Go Wrong

Investment risk gets all the attention during accumulation. "Will my portfolio grow enough? Can I handle the volatility?" But in retirement, the risks are different, more varied, and potentially more devastating if not properly managed.

### Longevity Risk: Living Longer Than Your Money

You might live to 95. Your spouse might live to 100. If you retire at 62, we're talking about potentially 40 years of retirement. Inflation alone will cut your purchasing power in half over that period. Healthcare costs will increase. Your spending patterns will change, often times with higher medical costs later, lower travel costs, but potentially catastrophic long-term care expenses.

How do retirement income specialists address longevity risk? Through a combination of guaranteed income sources and growth portfolios.

Social Security provides a baseline. Some clients benefit from annuitizing a portion of their portfolio to create an income floor, where they have enough to cover basic expenses regardless of what markets do. This might be through in-plan 401(k) income options, QLACs that start paying at 80 or 85, or immediate annuities.

The rest of the portfolio stays invested for growth to maintain purchasing power over decades. This isn't about maximizing returns. It's about balancing the need for guaranteed income (to sleep at night) with growth investments (to maintain lifestyle over 30+ years).

An interesting side about this, is that doing so allows you to take *more* investment risk with the other assets since you've now covered your essential expenses.

**Sequence of Returns Risk: The Timing of Returns Matters**

We've covered this in previous chapters, but it's worth reiterating: the order in which returns occur matters enormously when you're taking withdrawals. A market crash in your first few years of retirement can be devastating because you're forced to sell shares at depressed prices to generate income.

Retirement income specialists manage this through systematic withdrawal policies. Not "stay the course and keep withdrawing," but frameworks that specify: "When markets drop more than x%, we do a, b, and c."

The difference between having this framework in place versus making emotional decisions during crises is often the difference between a sustainable retirement and one that falls short.

**Healthcare and Long-Term Care Costs**

If you retire before 65, you need a bridge strategy to Medicare. This might be COBRA, ACA marketplace insurance, or coverage through a spouse still working. The costs can be substantial, for example, $1,500 to $2,000 per month or more, and need to be factored into your income plan.

Anecdotally, the number one reason I've seen clients continue to work is for health care until they turn 65.

At 65, you face Medicare decisions that many people don't often understand. Original Medicare with Medigap supplemental insurance, or Medicare Advantage? Part D drug coverage? These decisions affect both your costs and your coverage.

Long-term care is the expense most people don't want to think about. Traditional long-term care insurance has become expensive and is "use it or lose it", if you never need care, you've paid premiums for nothing.

Hybrid life insurance policies with long-term care riders have become increasingly popular, and here's why: you're guaranteed to get value from the policy in one of three ways.

First, you can access the cash value if you need it during your lifetime. The policy builds cash value that you can borrow against or withdraw.

Second, if you need long-term care, you can tap into a multiple of the death benefit for care expenses. For example, a $500,000 death benefit policy might have a 3x rider, giving you access to $1.5 million for long-term care costs.

Third, if you never need the cash value and never need long-term care, your beneficiaries receive the full death benefit when you pass away.

One option many people don't realize: if you have an existing whole life insurance policy you no longer need for its original purpose, you can often transfer it into one of these hybrid policies through a 1035 exchange. No tax consequences, and you've converted a policy that might have just sat there into one with long-term care protection.

The question of whether to buy a traditional LTC policy, use a hybrid product, or self-insure requires analysis of your overall financial situation, your family health history, and your risk tolerance. But the hybrid approach has become attractive because it's not wasted premium. You or your beneficiaries will receive value from it regardless of whether you need care.

### Estate Planning Integration

Estate planning isn't separate from retirement income planning. It's integrated throughout.

Beneficiary designations matter enormously. I've seen all the usual mistakes: men who remarried but still had their mother listed on old 401(k) accounts, ex-spouses still named, accounts not properly titled in the name of trusts, even though they paid the lawyer to create the documents.

But beyond fixing errors, strategic estate planning considers: Should your kids inherit your Roth accounts (tax-free) while charities get pre-tax IRA money (they don't pay taxes anyway)? Should you gift appreciated stock to adult children or hold it for step-up basis at death? How does the

SECURE Act's elimination of the stretch IRA affect your legacy planning?

These decisions affect both your retirement income strategy and your estate plan. They need to be coordinated, not handled in isolation.

## The Non-Financial Side That Most Advisors Ignore

Let me take a short detour and tell you about my own parents' retirement, because it illustrates something important that most growth-focused advisors never discuss: housing decisions and lifestyle planning.

My parents retired with a solid financial plan. Portfolio looked great. Income projections made sense. But nobody helped them think through where they actually wanted to live in retirement.

For 30 years, they'd lived in the same house in Wisconsin. They knew they wanted to spend winters somewhere warm, but that was about as far as the planning went.

So they started experimenting.

**Years one and two:** VRBOs in different Florida locations. It was nice, but too short-term to really know if they'd like living somewhere full-time.

**Year three**: they bought a house in Sarasota. They loved the area, loved the weather. But the neighborhood was well-established, and they quickly realized that making friends in your sixties in a community where everyone has lived there for 20 years is really hard. They felt isolated.

**Year four**: they sold the Sarasota house and built in a 55+ community that was still being developed. Completely different experience with new neighbors arriving regularly and built-in social activities. A community designed for their life stage. My Dad says it's one of the best retirement planning decisions he's made.

Then they made another move: they sold the Wisconsin house they'd lived in for three decades and built a new place closer to where my family lives. Closer to their longtime friend groups (and golf courses). Closer to the medical facilities.

Each of these decisions had significant financial implications. We're talking hundreds of thousands of dollars in real estate transactions. Potential capital gains taxes. Moving costs. The carrying cost of owning two homes while trying to sell one.

But more importantly, the first few years of their retirement, what should have been their most active "go-go" years, were spent figuring out where they wanted to be.

That's time you don't get back. Thankfully, it all worked out, but they wished they had spent more time experimenting with locations before they retired.

Could a financial planner have helped them avoid this expensive trial-and-error? Probably not a generalist advisor focused on investment management. But a retirement income specialist trained in comprehensive retirement planning? Absolutely.

This is part of what I call the "psychology of retirement."

These conversations should happen before you retire:

- Where do you see yourself living? Is that based on actual experience or fantasy?
- Have you spent time there in different seasons?
- What's your social network? How will you build community?
- Proximity to family: does it matter to you?
- Healthcare access as you age?
- One home or two? If two, what are the financial and logistical implications?
- When you're 85, where do you want to be? I wouldn't get too caught up on that at age 65, but it's worth contemplating.

A specialist helps you think through these questions systematically, and might even connect you with other clients who've made similar moves so you can learn from their experiences.

The financial pieces matter too: When do you sell your current home? Before or after establishing residency in a new state, if you're moving? How do you handle capital gains? If you're moving from Wisconsin to Florida, the timing affects your state taxes. If you're buying in a new location, how does that affect your cash flow and portfolio withdrawals?

My parents are now in their mid-seventies, and they're thriving. The housing decisions they eventually made have been crucial to their quality of life. But I watched them spend four years and probably thousands of dollars in moving and transaction costs, not to mention stress, figuring it out.

Some retirement income specialists are trained in these lifestyle planning conversations. They understand that retirement satisfaction isn't just about portfolio returns. It's about purpose, social connections, housing, relationships, health, and the psychological transition from career to retirement.

This will be covered more extensively in another book, but it's worth noting here: the financial aspect is just one part of successful retirement. Growth-focused advisors focus

100% on investments. The best retirement income specialists understand the bigger picture.

## How It All Comes Together: A Real Case Study

Let me walk you through a real client situation (details changed for privacy) to show how all of these pieces connect.

Meet Carol, age 64, recently widowed

Carol came to see me six months after her husband passed away unexpectedly. Unfortunately, many of my client relationships start this way.

She had about $1.8 million in assets:

$1.2 million in an IRA (rolled over from her late husband's 401(k))

$400,000 in a taxable brokerage account

$200,000 in a Roth IRA

For Social Security, her own benefit based on her work history would be about $1,800 per month. But she was eligible for a survivor benefit of $2,500 per month based on her late husband's earnings record.

She wanted to maintain her current lifestyle, which required about $90,000 per year. She was thinking about staying in Wisconsin for now but potentially moving to a condo in Florida to be closer to her golf friends. She was concerned about healthcare costs and the possibility of needing long-term care. And she wanted to leave something for her two daughters.

Here's what an accumulation advisor might say:

"You have $1.8 million. You can safely withdraw 4%, which is $72,000 per year, and increase it with inflation. Add in Social Security of $30,000, and you have $102,000 total annual income. You're in good shape."

Here's what I actually did as a retirement income specialist:

**Income strategy**: Carol's Social Security situation required careful analysis. As a widow, she had choices. She could claim survivor benefits based on her late husband's earnings immediately, or she could claim her own benefit first and preserve the higher survivor benefit for later.

Her own benefit at full retirement age (67) would be $1,800 per month. The survivor benefit at her full retirement age would be $2,500 per month, which was100% of what her husband was receiving.

Here's what we did: Carol claimed her own reduced retirement benefit at age 64, receiving about $1,500 per month. At age 67, when she reaches full retirement age, she'll switch to the survivor benefit of $2,500 per month.

Why this approach? By taking her smaller benefit first and delaying the survivor benefit until her full retirement age, she receives income now while preserving the maximum survivor benefit for when she switches at 67. Since the survivor benefit doesn't grow with delayed retirement credits past full retirement age, there's no advantage to waiting longer.

This meant for the first three years, she needed about $72,000 per year from her portfolio ($90,000 lifestyle minus $18,000 from Social Security). After age 67, when the survivor benefit kicked in at $30,000 per year, she needed only $60,000 annually from the portfolio.

**Tax planning**: Ages 64 through 72 are her golden Roth conversion years. She's in a relatively low tax bracket. We're converting $50,000 to $75,000 per year from the traditional IRA to her Roth, keeping her under the IRMAA threshold so her Medicare premiums don't spike.

By the time she reaches 73 and required minimum distributions begin, her traditional IRA will be much smaller. Her RMDs won't push her into high tax brackets or trigger Medicare surcharges. Over her retirement, this strategy will save her an estimated $150,000 in taxes.

**Healthcare**: She went on Medicare at 65. We modeled different Medicare supplement options and Part D prescription drug plans. We're budgeting $15,000 per year for healthcare costs, which will increase over time.

For long-term care, we analyzed several options. Carol decided to purchase a hybrid life insurance policy with a long-term care rider. $300,000 death benefit, with a 3x multiplier for long-term care expenses if needed, giving her access to $900,000 for care. If she never needs it, her daughters inherit the $300,000 death benefit. And we were able to fund this with an old whole life policy she had for years.

**Estate planning**: We updated her beneficiary designations. Her two daughters will inherit the Roth accounts (completely tax-free to them). The remaining traditional IRA, if any, at her death, will go to charity (which doesn't pay taxes anyway). This maximizes the tax efficiency of her legacy.

**Florida planning**: If Carol moves to Florida at age 69 as she's considering, we'll establish Florida domicile before doing any large Roth conversions that year. Wisconsin will scrutinize the move since she's lived there her whole life, so we'll be strategic about timing and documentation.

**Withdrawal strategy**: For the first few years, Carol is living primarily from her taxable account, letting the IRA and Roth grow. This minimizes her taxable income, keeps her in low brackets for the Roth conversions, and preserves the Roth for later when required minimum distributions might push her income higher. If the taxable account gets depleted, we'll shift to strategic IRA withdrawals coordinated with the ongoing Roth conversion strategy.

The result: Same $90,000 annual lifestyle. But with integrated planning across income, taxes, healthcare, long-term care, estate planning, and potential relocation, Carol will save more than $150,000 in lifetime taxes, her daughters will inherit more efficiently, she's protected against long-term care costs, and she has a clear roadmap for the next 30 years.

This is what comprehensive retirement income planning looks like. Not portfolio management with a 4% withdrawal assumption. A coordinated strategy across every aspect of retirement that matters.

Losing her husband was stressful beyond belief, but now she feels like she has a plan, and she can get back to living her retirement, even if it's different from what she originally envisioned.

## Why This Requires Specialized Training

The RICP® program I helped to create, teach, and direct at The American College of Financial Services covers 18 distinct competencies across retirement income planning. We go deep into Social Security claiming strategies, tax-efficient distribution planning, healthcare and Medicare navigation, pension analysis, risk management, estate planning integration, and the behavioral and psychological aspects of retirement transitions, and many more.

Most growth-focused, generalist advisors have studied three or four of these areas, and usually only at a surface level as part of broader CFP® curriculum. That's not a criticism of CFP® training which is excellent for comprehensive financial planning across all life stages. But it's not specialized retirement income training. I think of it as being broad, not deep.

The difference shows up in real money and real quality of life. Carol's planning will save her well over $150,000 compared to a generic "manage the portfolio and take 4%" approach. My parents would have saved years of trial-and-error and tens of thousands in transaction costs with better housing and lifestyle planning upfront. That couple with $5 million would have protected the wife's survivor benefit with better Social Security analysis.

These aren't minor optimizations. They're major financial and lifestyle outcomes that require specialized knowledge to get right.

In the next chapter, we'll look at the flip side: the dangerous defaults that growth-focused advisors use when they don't have this specialized training. Because what's worse than missing opportunities? Actively making mistakes that cost you money and compromise your retirement security.

## The Bottom Line

You don't need an investment manager in retirement. You need someone who can orchestrate income from multiple sources, minimize taxes across three decades, protect against a range of risks that didn't exist during your working years, and help you make housing and lifestyle decisions that affect both your finances and your quality of life.

That's not portfolio management. That's retirement income planning. And it's a specialization for a reason.

**Key Takeaways:**

- **Retirement income planning is about sustainable income, not portfolio returns.** The primary question shifts from "how do I grow this money?" to "can I afford my lifestyle without working?" This requires coordinating multiple income sources, like Social Security, portfolio withdrawals, pensions, part-time work, each with different tax treatments and strategic implications.

- **Tax planning becomes a 30-year optimization strategy.** Ages 62-72 often provide the golden window for Roth conversions before RMDs begin. Strategic withdrawal sequencing across pre-tax, Roth, and taxable accounts can save six figures in lifetime taxes. Medicare IRMAA thresholds, qualified charitable distributions, and bracket management require sophisticated multi-year modeling.

- **Comprehensive planning addresses both financial and life transitions.** Housing decisions, healthcare planning, long-term care funding, estate planning integration, and the psychological transition from accumulation to spending all require specialized knowledge. The best retirement income specialists understand both the technical financial side and the behavioral aspects of this major life transition.

# Chapter 5: The Dangerous Defaults A Generalist Advisor Uses

*"It ain't what you don't know that gets you into trouble. It's what you know for sure that just ain't so."*

— Mark Twain (attributed)

When Robert and Susan came to see me, they brought their "comprehensive retirement income plan" from their current advisor.

It was 72 pages long.

Robert seemed almost apologetic. "I know this looks like a lot. Our advisor spent two meetings going through it with us. But I have to be honest, I still don't really understand what it's telling us."

I started flipping through it. Page after page of charts, projections, graphs showing their portfolio growing over time under different scenarios. It looked impressively thorough.

But as I read more carefully, I started seeing the same numbers appearing repeatedly: 3% inflation assumption on every page. Age 92 listed as their life expectancy, despite Susan being four years younger and having better health. Returns shown as fixed growth, 8% this year, 8% next year, 8% the year after. Their spending needs calculated as exactly 80% of their pre-retirement income, increased by exactly 3% every single year for 30 years.

"Can I ask you something?" I said. "Did he talk to you about what inflation rate to use? Or did he just use 3%?"

Robert and Susan looked at each other. "He didn't ask," Susan said. "Is 3% wrong?"

"It's not that it's wrong. It's that it's a default. It's what the software uses unless someone changes it. Same question: did he discuss how long you might live? Why both of you are assumed to die at exactly 92?"

"He didn't," Robert said. "The software just... calculated that, I guess?"

"And your spending, did you talk through what you'll actually spend in your 60s versus your 70s versus your 80s?

Whether you have big one-time expenses planned? How healthcare costs might be different from other expenses?"

"Not really," Susan admitted. "He asked what we spend now, and then said we'd need about 80% of that in retirement since we won't be saving anymore or paying payroll taxes."

That's when I knew what I was looking at. This wasn't a customized retirement income plan. It was 72 pages of default assumptions run through planning software. It looked comprehensive. It was professionally formatted. It had impressive-looking charts and projections.

But it was built on generic inputs that had nothing to do with Robert and Susan's actual situation, their specific goals, or the complex realities they'd face across 30 years of retirement.

And here's what made it particularly concerning: Robert and Susan's advisor probably believed he'd done thorough work. He'd spent hours in the software. He'd generated detailed projections. He'd reviewed it with them across two meetings.

He just didn't know what he didn't know.

## Why Many Advisors Rely on Defaults

Before we get into the specific defaults, let's understand why they persist.

Many advisors aren't deliberately trying to give you cookie-cutter plans. They're doing what they've been trained to do. And their training focused almost exclusively on accumulation: building portfolios, managing risk during the growth phase, and helping clients save consistently.

When those same advisors encounter retirement planning, they apply what they know. They use the planning software they have. They rely on the "rules of thumb" they learned. They assume the same approaches that worked during accumulation will work during retirement.

The software encourages this. Most financial planning programs come pre-loaded with default assumptions: 80% income replacement, 3% inflation, specific withdrawal rates, standard allocation models. Changing these defaults requires understanding why they might not fit a specific client's situation.

If you've never been trained in specialized retirement income planning, you don't know what to change or why.

It's also faster to use templates. A customized retirement income plan requires extensive analysis: detailed spending projections by phase, tax modeling across multiple years, Social Security optimization, withdrawal sequencing strategies, stress testing for various scenarios. That might take 20-30 hours of work. Plugging numbers into software with default assumptions takes 2-3 hours.

Most importantly, advisors often don't recognize the limitations of their approach. During accumulation, one-size-fits-most actually works reasonably well. Everyone's trying to grow their portfolio. The strategies are similar. Market returns drive most of the outcome.

**But retirement income planning is different.** *Your* spending pattern matters. *Your* tax situation matters. *Your* other income sources matter. *Your* health, housing plans, legacy goals, risk tolerance and preferences for guarantees versus flexibility, all of these create meaningful differences in what strategies make sense.

Generalist advisors don't see these differences as significant variables requiring customized strategies. They see them as details that don't fundamentally change the approach.

That's the gap. Not malice. Not incompetence. Just the natural result of applying non-specialized training to retirement income challenges.

## The One-Size-Fits-All Problem

Here's what generalist advisors miss: every retirement is fundamentally different in ways that matter enormously for planning.

Two couples with identical $2 million portfolios might need completely different strategies based on:

**Spending patterns.** One couple plans a consistent $90,000 annually. Another wants $120,000 in their 60s for aggressive travel, dropping to $75,000 in their 80s. A third has lumpy spending: $80,000 baseline but needs $40,000 every three years for a new car, $60,000 eventually for a kitchen remodel, and a potential $25,000 annually to help grandchildren with college.

**Health and longevity expectations.** One person has a family history of longevity and excellent health. Another has serious health conditions and may not reach average life expectancy. These aren't just emotional factors. They drive decisions about Social Security timing, spending rates, and how much to allocate to guaranteed income.

**Other income sources**. One retiree has a $30,000 pension covering baseline needs. Another has $50,000 in rental income, but it comes with management headaches. A third has no pension but a significant part-time consulting income for the first five years of retirement. Each situation changes how you structure portfolio withdrawals.

**Legacy goals.** One couple wants to maximize their lifestyle with minimal inheritance. Another prioritizes leaving substantial assets to children. A third cares deeply about charitable giving. These goals affect everything from Roth conversion strategies to withdrawal sequencing to life insurance planning.

**Risk tolerance.** Not just for market volatility, but for income certainty. Some people are comfortable with spending flexibility, adjusting based on portfolio performance. Others need to know exactly what their income will be. Some are fine spending down to zero. Others want absolute certainty they won't outlive their money even if they live to 100.

**Tax situations.** One couple has $1.8 million in traditional IRAs, virtually nothing in Roth. Another has balanced across pre-tax, Roth, and taxable accounts. A third has significant taxable accounts with low basis. These differences create completely different optimal withdrawal strategies.

**Housing plans**. Staying put in a paid-off home? Downsizing and freeing up equity? Relocating to a lower-cost or no-tax state? Buying a second home? Each has different financial implications for portfolio withdrawals, tax planning, and overall strategy.

Generalist advisors treat these differences as interesting background information. They acknowledge them, maybe adjust the withdrawal rate by half a percent, and then apply essentially the same template.

Retirement income specialists treat these differences as the foundation of the plan. The strategy flows from your specific situation, not from a generic model.

Let me show you what this looks like in practice by walking through the most common defaults.

## Default #1: The 80% "Replacement" Ratio

Many advisors say, "You'll need 80% of your pre-retirement income in retirement."

Once you dig into this a little, it's easy to see there are several problems with this assumption.

**Problem one: You should be replacing *expenses*, not *income*.**

If a surgeon earns $400,000 but has been living on $200,000 (investing or saving the rest), they don't need

$320,000 in retirement (80% of income). They need $200,000, which is what they were actually spending on their lifestyle.

The 80% replacement ratio looks at what you earned, not what you spent. For high earners who save aggressively, this drastically overestimates retirement needs. For people who spent everything they made, it might be closer. But the "rule" doesn't make that distinction.

**Problem two: The 80% rule ignores that spending often changes in phases.**

Research shows that retirement spending isn't flat. It often follows a pattern:

**Go-go years (roughly ages 65-75):** Often higher spending than working years. You're healthy, active, traveling, pursuing hobbies, helping grandchildren, and checking off bucket list items. Many clients need 95-110% of their working lifestyle expenses during this phase, not 80%. Some need more because they're finally doing things they deferred during their career.

**Slow-go years (roughly ages 75-85):** Spending moderates. Less travel, more predictable routine, fewer big purchases. This phase might actually hit that 70-80% target.

**No-go years (85+):** Baseline lifestyle spending drops significantly. Less travel, simpler life. But healthcare costs spike. And if long-term care is needed, costs can be $8,000-$15,000 monthly, completely overwhelming the "80% of income" calculation.

**Problem three: One-time lumpy expenses don't fit the replacement ratio model.**

Replacing vehicles every 7-10 years. New appliances. Roof repairs. HVAC replacement. Major home maintenance. Helping adult children during financial stress. Contributing to grandchildren's education.

These aren't annual recurring expenses that fit neatly into a replacement ratio. But they're real costs that need to be funded from your portfolio.

Let me give you a real example.

Client earned $155,000, contributed $25,000 annually to 401(k), lived on $130,000. Their generalist advisor assumed the 80% rule: plan for $124,000 annually in retirement (80% of $155,000).

We did a detailed expense analysis instead:

**Ages 65-72 (go-go years):** $145,000 annually. More travel than during working years, season tickets they'd always wanted, annual family vacations with kids and grandkids, home improvements they'd deferred.

**Ages 73-80 (slow-go):** $110,000 annually. Travel drops off, lifestyle becomes more predictable, fewer big expenditures.

**Ages 81+ (no-go):** $95,000 baseline lifestyle spending, but separate modeling for potential long-term care costs of $120,000-180,000 annually if needed.

**Plus lumpy expenses:** New car every eight years ($45,000), major home updates ($80,000 over 10 years), helping grandchildren with college ($15,000 annually for six years).

Importantly, these were all inflation-adjusted amounts.

The 80% replacement ratio would have significantly underfunded their early retirement years and completely missed the lumpy expenses. By doing actual expense planning rather than applying a generic rule, we built a plan that matched their real life.

The retirement income specialist approach: Model actual spending categories, allow spending to vary by phase, budget separately for one-time expenses and healthcare, and revisit assumptions regularly as retirement unfolds.

## Default #2: "The 4% Rule"

The biggest problem with the 4% rule isn't that it's wrong, *per se*. It's that advisors treat it as the answer when it's just *one* approach among many.

Let me be clear about what the so-called "4% rule" actually is: It came from William Bengen's research in the 1990s. He analyzed every possible 30-year retirement period in U.S. market history going back to 1926. For each period, he calculated the maximum withdrawal rate that would have allowed the portfolio to survive the full 30 years.

The worst 30-year period? Retiring in 1966. High inflation, poor stock returns, brutal sequence. Even in that worst historical period, a 4% starting withdrawal rate (adjusted annually for inflation) would have kept the portfolio from running out.

Bengen called this the "safe maximum" withdrawal rate—SAFEMAX. It wasn't about probability. It was about the historical worst case. If you could survive retiring in 1966, you could survive anything history had thrown at retirees.

But here's what most people miss: 4% wasn't the average sustainable rate. It wasn't the comfortable rate. It was the maximum rate that survived the *worst*-case scenario. Many retirement periods could have supported much higher withdrawals, causing many people to underspend and enjoy their retirement.

And Bengen's research was based on a specific portfolio: a mix of U.S. stocks and intermediate-term Treasury bonds. It didn't account for international diversification, different asset allocations, or various other factors that have been studied since. Or what about 35 years, or 40 years of retirement? See the issue?

Bottom line: it's not a rule. It's one of several strategies in the retirement income playbook.

Other strategies that retirement income specialists may consider:

- Fixed dollar with inflation adjustments
- Flooring or safety-first methods
- Guardrail systems
- Time segmentation or bucketing strategies
- Probability-based withdrawal rates
- The RMD method
- Dividend strategies

Here's the critical point: Different strategies work for different situations.

Most advisors default to "4% adjusted for inflation" because that's what they know. It's simple. It's defensible. Software makes it easy to calculate.

Retirement income specialists choose the withdrawal strategy that fits your situation: your risk tolerance, your spending flexibility, your other income sources, your goals, and your psychological comfort with uncertainty.

There's no universal "best" withdrawal strategy. The right answer depends on understanding your complete picture and designing a strategy around it.

## Default #3: "Always Withdraw Taxable First" Without Analyzing What That Means for You

Many advisors learn a withdrawal sequence: "Take from taxable accounts first, then pre-tax IRAs, then Roth accounts last."

The logic sounds reasonable. Taxable accounts have capital gains treatment (lower tax rates than ordinary income). Roth accounts are tax-free forever, so preserve them as long as possible. Pre-tax IRAs fall in the middle.

But this is also a default that can be wrong for your specific situation.

If you follow "taxable first" blindly, here's what happens: You spend down all your taxable accounts in your 60s and early 70s while your traditional IRA sits untouched and continues growing. At age 73, required minimum distributions begin. Suddenly, you're forced to take large taxable distributions whether you need the money or not.

Your tax bracket spikes. Your Medicare Part B and Part D premiums increase (IRMAA surcharges can add $5,000+ annually). You're paying far more in lifetime taxes than necessary. And your kids will eventually inherit a large pre-tax IRA that creates a significant tax burden for them.

The right withdrawal sequence depends on your specific situation:

What's your current tax bracket? If you're in the 12% bracket now but will be in the 24% bracket once RMDs start, you want to be pulling money from the traditional IRA now (or doing Roth conversions) even if you don't need it for spending.

Are you doing Roth conversions? If so, your entire withdrawal sequence changes. You might live primarily on your taxable account while systematically converting traditional IRA money to Roth, intentionally keeping yourself in a specific tax bracket.

Are you near Medicare IRMAA thresholds? If your modified adjusted gross income is close to the threshold ($206,000 for joint filers in 2024), the source of your withdrawals can determine whether you pay standard Medicare premiums or significantly higher ones.

Do you have charitable giving plans? If you're charitably inclined and over 70½, qualified charitable distributions (QCDs) from your IRA are powerful. They satisfy your RMD but don't count as taxable income. This might mean touching your IRA earlier than the "taxable first" rule suggests.

What do you want your kids to inherit? Roth accounts pass to heirs tax-free. Pre-tax IRAs create a tax burden for them (they have to withdraw it within 10 years under current rules). If legacy planning matters, you might intentionally convert more to Roth even if it means higher taxes for you, because it creates tax-free inheritance for your children.

There's no universal "best" withdrawal sequence. The right answer requires comprehensive tax planning across your entire retirement, accounting for your current situation, your future situation, Medicare considerations, estate planning goals, and charitable intentions.

## Default #4: Planning for "Average" Returns and Not Understanding Variation

Here's one of the most dangerous assumptions most advisors make: "The stock market averages 10% annually" (or 8%, or 7%, depending on what time period and data they're using), "so we'll plan for average returns in your retirement."

The problem isn't that the *average* return is not the *annual* return. Even if stocks average 8% per year, it's not a straight line return. A famous investor promised his clients 8% per year with no fluctuation. His name was Bernie Madoff!

You don't get the average every year. You get variation. Sometimes large variation.

Some years are up 30%. Some are down 18%. Some are up 6%. Some are down 22%. Some are up 22%. The average over 30 years might be 8%, but you will never actually experience a year that's exactly 8%. That "average" is a statistical artifact, not a reality you'll live through.

This is what generalist advisors miss: variation is what matters in retirement, not the average.

During accumulation, variation actually helps you through dollar-cost averaging. When you're adding money every paycheck, market declines let you buy more shares at lower prices. When markets surge, your earlier purchases benefit. Bad years early actually improve your long-term outcome because you're purchasing shares cheaply. Over 30 years of contributions, the sequence of returns doesn't matter nearly as much.

**In retirement, variation destroys you if it comes at the wrong time.**

If you retire and immediately experience two years of negative returns while you're taking withdrawals from investments to live on, you're selling shares at depressed prices. Those shares can be very difficult to recover because they're gone. You spent them on groceries, housing, healthcare, and life. Even if the market subsequently recovers and your long-term average return is fine, you've permanently reduced the portfolio that needs to support you for the next 25 years.

This is the "sequence of returns risk" we've discussed earlier, and it's why planning for "average returns" is dangerous.

Dave Ramsey famously got criticized for suggesting people could withdraw 8% annually because "the stock market averages 8% returns." Financial planners across the country pointed out why this is dangerous: you don't get 8% every year like clockwork. You get variation. And if the negative variation comes early in your retirement while you're withdrawing 8%, you will almost certainly run out of money.

The same problem exists with inflation assumptions. Most advisors plug in "3% average inflation" and move on. But healthcare inflation runs 5-7% annually. Housing costs vary by location. We just lived through a period where general inflation spiked to 8-9%. Planning for a smooth 3% progression misses the reality of variation, especially if high inflation hits early in your retirement when your assets haven't had time to grow.

**Retirement income specialists stress-test for variation:**

- What if returns are below average for the first 10 years of your retirement? Does your plan still work?
- What if we experience a 2008-style crash (50% decline) in your third year of retirement? How does that affect your sustainability?
- What if inflation spikes to 7-8% for five years early in your retirement? Can your portfolio keep up?
- What if returns and inflation both disappoint simultaneously? This is the worst case, but it happens (see the 1970s).

This isn't pessimism. It's preparedness. If your plan only works with average returns happening in a favorable sequence, you don't actually have a plan. You have a hope dressed up as a projection.

The great thing about doing this is that you feel more confident in your plan before retiring, and that's the whole point!

Planning for average returns is like planning a cross-country drive by assuming you'll hit all green lights. It's technically possible, but it's not how the world works. You need a plan for the red lights.

## Default #5: "The Plan Is Done"

Here's perhaps the most dangerous default of all: treating retirement planning as a one-time event.

Generalist advisors create a plan for your retirement, says "you're all set," and then just sends quarterly portfolio performance reports. Maybe an annual review where you look at account balances and reaffirm the strategy. But no proactive monitoring of whether the plan is still on track. No systematic adjustments as circumstances change. Just portfolio statements.

The problem: things change and plans must evolve.

**External changes you can't control:**

Market returns differ from projections, sometimes dramatically. The first decade of your retirement might see below-average returns. Or above-average. Or massive volatility. Your plan needs to adapt.

Inflation varies. We just lived through this. Everyone who retired in 2019 with "3% inflation assumption" plans watched their actual costs increase 8-9% annually in 2021-2023. Healthcare inflation consistently runs above general inflation. Your plan needs to account for actual inflation, not projected.

Tax laws change constantly. The SECURE Act in 2019 changed RMD ages and eliminated stretch IRAs for most beneficiaries. SECURE 2.0 in 2022 changed RMD ages again and modified catch-up contribution rules. Tax rates themselves change with new administrations and Congressional actions. Your plan needs to adapt to the current rules, not the rules from 2019.

Healthcare costs and Medicare rules change. Medicare premiums increase. IRMAA thresholds adjust. Drug costs change. Long-term care insurance options evolve. Your plan needs to reflect current healthcare realities.

Interest rates shift dramatically. The decade from 2010-2020 saw historically low rates. Then rapid increases in 2022-

2023. This affects everything from bond returns to annuity pricing to mortgage decisions if you're downsizing.

**Internal changes specific to you:**

Health changes, better or worse than expected. Maybe you're healthier at 75 than you anticipated and want to increase travel spending. Or health issues emerge requiring different planning.

Family situations evolve. Adult children face financial stress and need help. Grandchildren's education becomes a priority. A parent needs care. These aren't predictable at retirement but they're common and they affect your plan.

You decide to move, downsize, or buy a second home. Housing changes have major financial implications: capital gains on home sale, cost of new location, ongoing expenses, potential rental income. Your withdrawal strategy needs to accommodate these changes.

Your spouse passes away. This completely changes the financial picture: survivor benefits, tax filing status (single vs. joint), different RMDs, healthcare costs for one person, potentially different housing situation. Your plan needs rebuilding, not just minor adjustments.

Your spending patterns change. You travel less than you expected (or more). Healthcare costs are higher (or lower).

You become more (or less) interested in legacy planning. Your actual lifestyle might differ from what you projected at retirement.

Your priorities evolve. At 65, maximizing your lifestyle might be paramount. At 75, after a health scare, legacy planning might become more important. At 85, simplification and reducing stress might outweigh optimization. Your plan should evolve with your priorities.

A retirement income specialist doesn't just create a plan and walk away. They monitor continuously and adjust proactively:

Annual comprehensive reviews. Not just "here's your performance versus benchmarks," but "let's stress-test whether the plan still works given everything that's changed this year. Are we on track? Do we need adjustments?"

Proactive tax planning updates. When tax laws change or your situation changes, Roth conversion strategies might need updating. Withdrawal sequencing might need adjusting. Charitable giving approaches might need revisiting. QCD strategies at 70½. Coordination with your CPA throughout the year, not just at tax time.

Spending adjustments, upward or downward. If markets significantly underperform in your early retirement years, discuss temporary spending reductions and show exactly how that improves long-term sustainability. If markets significantly outperform, discuss spending increases or enhanced legacy planning. The plan should be dynamic, not static.

Strategy pivots when appropriate. Maybe the withdrawal strategy needs changing from fixed percentage to guardrails-based. Maybe guaranteed income becomes more attractive as you age. Maybe housing plans shift and require different positioning.

Monitoring external factors. When inflation spikes, immediately assess impact on your plan. When tax laws change, analyze implications for your strategy. When interest rates move dramatically, review whether annuity pricing has become more attractive. When healthcare costs change, update projections.

Retirement income planning isn't a "product" you buy once. When done well, it's an ongoing advisory relationship that adapts your strategy as your life and the world change. The plan you create at age 65 won't be the plan you're using at age 75, and it shouldn't be. Life evolves. Markets evolve. Rules evolve. Your plan needs to evolve with them.

## Why This Matters More Than You Think

These defaults don't just cost you money, though they absolutely do. Suboptimal planning easily costs six figures over a 30-year retirement through unnecessary taxes, missed Social Security optimization, and poor withdrawal sequencing.

But the deeper costs are harder to quantify and perhaps more important:

**Confidence.** With a plan built on generic defaults and best-case assumptions, you don't really know if you'll be okay. You have a projection that says "85% probability of success," but you don't understand what that means or what you should do in the 15% of scenarios where things don't work out. Every market downturn triggers anxiety because you don't have a framework for whether you should be adjusting or staying the course.

**Flexibility.** Without knowing your actual spending capacity across different phases and market conditions, you can't make informed decisions about helping your kids, buying that second home, splurging on that big trip, or increasing your charitable giving. You're either overly cautious (leaving opportunities on the table) or overly aggressive (taking risks you don't realize you're taking).

**Opportunity cost.** You're leaving money on the table through tax inefficiency, suboptimal Social Security claiming, and withdrawal strategies that don't fit your situation. Every year you delay proper retirement income planning is a year of missed Roth conversion opportunities, unnecessary IRMAA surcharges, or locked-in Social Security decisions that can't be reversed.

**Peace of mind.** This might be the biggest cost. With generic default planning, you're never quite sure if you're doing it right. Every financial decision comes with uncertainty and worry. Did we claim Social Security at the right time? Are we withdrawing from the right accounts? Should we be adjusting spending? Anxiety compounds over 30 years of retirement.

**The alternative, customized retirement income planning, provides clarity.** You understand your plan. You know what you can spend in different scenarios. You have a framework for making adjustments when needed. You're not wondering if you've missed something important because the planning was comprehensive from the start.

That's the difference between default-based planning and specialized retirement income planning. One is generic, reactive, and built on assumptions. The other is customized, proactive, and built on your specific situation.

**

In the next chapter, we'll look at the often-uncomfortable topic of how advisors get paid, what conflicts different compensation models create, and what you should know about fees, commissions, and alignment of interests.

Because understanding what drives your advisor's recommendations is crucial to evaluating whether you're getting specialized retirement income planning or just default-based advice.

## Key Takeaways:

- **Generic assumptions create expensive blind spots.** The 80% income replacement ratio, 4% withdrawal rule, 3% inflation assumption, and "always withdraw taxable first" sequencing are defaults that sound reasonable but often don't fit individual situations. These templates work for software demonstrations, not real retirements with lumpy spending, varying phases, and unique tax situations.

- **Planning for average returns ignores the variation that destroys sustainability.** During accumulation, averaging 8% annually works even with volatility because you're adding money. In retirement, the sequence matters enormously and negative returns early can permanently damage your portfolio because you're selling shares at depressed prices. Stress-testing for variation, not just projecting average returns, is essential.

- **Retirement planning isn't a one-time event, it's an ongoing process.** Markets change, tax laws change, health changes, family situations evolve, and priorities shift. A plan created at age 65 needs regular updating and adjustments as life unfolds. Accumulation-focused advisors often create a plan and then just monitor portfolio performance; retirement income specialists continuously optimize based on changing circumstances.

# Chapter 6: Understanding Advisor Compensation and Conflicts

*"It is difficult to get a man to understand something when his salary depends upon his not understanding it."*

— Upton Sinclair

When Tom came to see me, he brought a box of statements and documents from his current advisor. Literally, a large cardboard box.

"I pay a 1% advisory fee," he said. "That shows up on my quarterly invoice. Pretty straightforward. That's average, right?"

I started going through his statements. Within ten minutes, I'd found three layers of fees he had no idea he was paying.

"Let's start with these mutual funds," I said, pulling up his account statement. "You're holding five different funds here. Each one has its own internal expense ratio, basically, the fund company's annual fee for managing the fund. This one is charging 1.2% annually. This one is 0.9%. And this one..." I had to check it twice. "This floating rate fund is charging 2.5% per year."

Tom looked confused. "I thought the 1% I pay my advisor covered the fund management?"

"No, that's his fee for managing your account, like deciding which funds to buy. But then each fund charges its own fee on top of that. So you're paying his 1% plus another 1% to 1.5% in fund expenses. Total cost is over 2%."

"What the heck! I didn't know that!" Tom said.

I kept digging. "Now let's look at these trade confirmations." I pulled out a stack. "Your advisor is buying and selling stocks fairly frequently. See this? $250 commission to sell this stock. Another $250 to buy that one. Here's another trade with a $200 commission. These add up."

"Wait, I thought the 1% covered trading?"

"It does on your IRA and Roth accounts. Those are advisory fee accounts. But your taxable brokerage account is set up differently. You're being charged commissions on each trade. Did your advisor explain you had two different fee structures?"

Tom shook his head. "I knew I had different types of accounts. But I thought they all worked the same way."

"This is actually pretty common at some firms. Retirement accounts are on what is called an "advisory fee platform", and brokerage accounts are still transaction-based. But clients often don't realize they're paying different ways on different accounts." I added up the confirmations. "You paid about $2,800 in commissions last year on your brokerage account, on top of the 1% advisory fee on your retirement accounts."

Then I got to the annuity paperwork, a massive document that looked like a phone book. "Tell me about this annuity."

"My advisor recommended it eight years ago. He said it was safe, even if the market crashed, I couldn't lose money. And it would guarantee me income in retirement."

I started reading through the prospectus. Variable annuity. Multiple fee layers. "Okay, here's what you actually have. There's a mortality and expense charge. That's 1.2% annually. Then, the investment options inside the annuity, what they call sub-accounts, average about 1% in fees. And you have an optional income rider that costs another 0.6% per year."

Tom was doing the math in his head. "So the annuity is costing me 2.8% annually?"

"Yes. And about that 'can't lose money' part. That only applies to the income benefit. The actual account value can absolutely go down if the market drops. The guarantee is that once you turn on income, it won't decrease. But that's not the same as the account value being protected."

"I don't think that's how it was explained to me," Tom said quietly.

He sat back in his chair. "So between the advisory fee, the mutual fund expenses, the trading commissions, and the annuity fees, I'm paying..."

"It varies by account, but your total cost is probably 2.5% to 3% annually across your portfolio."

"Why didn't he tell me this?"

That's the question. And honestly, I don't think Tom's advisor was being deliberately deceptive. He works for a large, nationwide firm where this structure is standard. Multiple fee layers, products with embedded commissions, proprietary investments. It's just "how things work" there.

Unfortunately, I see Tom's story regularly with prospective clients.

The advisor probably mentioned some of this in passing during initial meetings. But without a clear, direct explanation of total costs and how all the pieces fit together, Tom had no idea what he was really paying.

And more importantly, he didn't understand the conflicts those different compensation structures created.

Some of those mutual fund expense ratios are high because the fund company pays revenue sharing back to the brokerage firm. The variable annuity paid the advisor a commission when Tom bought it eight years ago. The frequent trading generates commission revenue. None of this is necessarily illegal or unethical, but it creates incentives that might not align with Tom's best interests.

Here's my perspective: I don't care much about which fee model an advisor uses. What I care about is whether they're transparent about it, whether they understand the conflicts it creates, and whether they have the expertise to consistently act in your best interest despite those conflicts.

Let me walk you through the main ways advisors get paid, the conflicts each model creates, and how to evaluate whether your advisor is handling those conflicts appropriately.

## The Three Main Compensation Models

There are really three primary ways financial advisors are compensated, with variations within each.

### Commission-Based

The advisor is paid by product sales. When you buy a mutual fund, annuity, insurance policy, or investment, the advisor receives a commission from the company that issued the product. Some commissions are paid upfront (you buy an annuity, advisor gets 5% immediately). Others are paid over time as "trail commissions" (ex. you hold a mutual fund, advisor gets 0.25% annually).

**The potential conflict:** The advisor has an incentive to recommend products that pay higher commissions, whether or not they're optimal for you. They might also have an incentive to “churn” your investments (sell and buy new products) to generate new commissions.

**When it can work:** If the advisor is transparent about commissions, has genuine expertise, operates as a fiduciary (legally obligated to act in your best interest), and you're comfortable with the structure. Some products are only available on a commission basis, and some clients prefer paying for advice through product purchases rather than separate fees.

**Red flags:** Advisor won't clearly explain how they're paid. Frequent recommendations to change investments, like constantly buying and selling stocks on their "focus list". Emphasis on products rather than planning. Resistance to explaining why a specific product is appropriate for your situation.

### Assets Under Management (AUM)

The advisor charges an annual percentage fee based on the assets they manage for you. Typically 0.75% to 1.25% for most clients. The fee might be lower for very large accounts, or it might vary based on the scope of services provided. If the advisor is predominantly doing asset management with minimal other planning, the fee should be on the lower end. If they're providing comprehensive coordination (tax planning, healthcare strategy, estate planning coordination, working with your CPA and attorney, ongoing retirement income optimization), the fee reflects that broader scope of work.

If you have $1 million and your advisor charges 1%, you pay $10,000 per year. This fee is usually deducted quarterly from your account.

**The potential conflict:** The advisor benefits financially when your assets grow and loses income when assets decline or when you withdraw large sums. This could theoretically bias them toward keeping everything invested, even when other strategies (like using some assets for guaranteed income, paying off a mortgage, or gifting to children) might be appropriate.

**When it can work:** When the advisor provides comprehensive planning (not just investment management), aligns their success with yours (they make more when you do well), and is willing to recommend strategies that might reduce assets under management if those strategies are in your best interest. This model works well for clients who want ongoing planning and portfolio management as an integrated service.

**Red flags:** Advisor focuses exclusively on investment management, not comprehensive planning. Also uses high-fee investments in the portfolio, as explained in Tom's case previously. Dismisses any strategy that would reduce assets under management (paying off debt, charitable giving, guaranteed income products). Charges AUM fee but provides minimal service beyond quarterly performance reports.

This is the model we use at Stockbridge Private Wealth Management, and I'll explain how we think about it in a moment.

### Subscription or Fee-for-Service

The advisor charges a flat fee, either monthly (retainer) or per project (fee-for-service). This might be $5,000 per year for ongoing planning, or $3,000 for a one-time comprehensive retirement income plan. The fee is independent of your asset size or what products you use.

**The potential conflict:** The advisor's income doesn't increase if your portfolio grows, which could theoretically reduce their incentive to help you optimize investments. They might also have less incentive to check in regularly since their fee is the same regardless of how much time they spend with you. Some advisors charge very high hourly rates, which can make clients reluctant to call with questions.

**When it can work:** When you want advice but prefer to implement it yourself, when you have a complex situation requiring specialized planning, or when you want to separate planning advice from investment management. Can be good for do-it-yourself investors who need periodic guidance. At Stockbridge, we sometimes do a monthly subscription fee when a client is near retirement and wants to start an ongoing planning relationship, but is unable to move their investment accounts until they actually retire.

**Red flags:** Advisor provides a plan but little ongoing support. Charges significant fees but delivers minimal value. Hourly rates so high that clients avoid calling with questions.

## What Matters More Than the Fee Model

Here's the thing: every compensation model creates some potential conflict. There is no perfect, conflict-free structure.

Commission-based advisors might be tempted to recommend higher-commission products. AUM-based advisors might be tempted to keep all assets invested. Fee-only advisors might be tempted to minimize time spent once they've collected their fee.

What actually matters is:

**Expertise.** This should be first because it's the most important. Does your advisor have the specialized knowledge required for retirement income planning? The best fee structure in the world doesn't help if your advisor lacks expertise.

And here's something that surprises many people: the "cheaper" advisor often costs you far more in the long run.

Let me give you a concrete example from an actual conversation I had years ago with one of my highest net-worth clients.

He came to me after his previous advisor retired. "I need to tell you upfront," he said, "I'm paying 0.3% with my current guy. I know you charge more than that. I'm not sure I want to pay a higher fee."

Fair concern. From a pure cost comparison, his previous arrangement looked like a great deal.

"It's not what you pay necessarily, it's what you get for what you pay. Tell me about what you got for that 0.3%," I said.

"Portfolio management. He rebalances quarterly, sends performance reports, we meet once or twice a year to review things. And he trades bonds for me."

"Did he do retirement income planning? Help you think through Social Security timing, tax strategies, withdrawal sequencing?"

"Not really. He said those were personal decisions. He focused on managing the investments."

As we dug deeper, I discovered the real cost of that "good deal."

He'd claimed Social Security at 62 because he wanted to "invest it and come out ahead." His investment advisor never analyzed whether that was optimal given his situation, his wife's situation, or the value of the survivor benefit. He just said, "if you want to claim early, we can invest the money."

The client passed away at 72 from an unexpected illness. His early claiming decision meant his wife is now receiving a survivor benefit that's roughly $1,500 per month less than if he'd delayed to 70. Over her expected lifetime, that decision will cost her well over $200,000.

His previous investment advisor wasn't incompetent. He did exactly what he was hired to do: manage the portfolio efficiently at a low cost. He just wasn't a retirement income specialist. He didn't do comprehensive planning. He managed investments.

The point isn't that low fees are bad. The point is that focusing solely on the fee percentage misses the bigger question: what are you actually getting for that fee, and what's the cost of what you're not getting?

**Transparency.** Does your advisor clearly explain how they're compensated? Do you understand exactly what you're paying and what you're receiving for that payment? Are there any other payments the advisor receives that you should know about?

And here's something many clients miss: there's the fee you see and the fee you don't see. I've had dozens of meetings with prospective clients who knew they were paying a 1% advisory fee but had no idea they were also paying 1% in mutual fund expenses inside their portfolio. They thought their total cost was 1%, but it was actually 2%, like Tom's story.

The underlying investments matter too. Mutual funds often have higher expense ratios than ETFs and can be less tax-efficient, generating unnecessary capital gains distributions. Your advisor should be explaining not just their fee, but the total cost of your investment strategy including fund expenses. If they're using expensive mutual funds when low-cost ETFs would work better, you need to understand why and whether that decision is in your best interest or theirs.

**Fiduciary commitment.** Is your advisor legally obligated to act in your best interest 100% of the time? This matters more than fee structure. An AUM-based fiduciary who transparently explains conflicts and consistently acts in your interest is better than a commission-based advisor who isn't held to fiduciary standards.

**Demonstrated behavior.** Does your advisor actually recommend strategies that might reduce their compensation when those strategies are in your best interest? That's the test. If an AUM-based advisor recommends you pay off your mortgage with a lump sum from your portfolio (reducing their fee), or if a commission-based advisor steers you away from a high-commission product because it's not right for you, those are good signs.

## How We Handle This at Our Firm

Since I'm asking you to evaluate how your advisor handles compensation and conflicts, let me be transparent about our approach.

We use an AUM-based fee structure. We charge a percentage of assets we manage, typically 0.25% per quarter, and is lower for higher account values. That fee covers comprehensive retirement income planning and ongoing portfolio management.

I'm aware of the potential conflicts this creates. Here's how we handle them:

**We don't charge separately for planning.** Many AUM-based advisors charge a separate planning fee (often $2,500-$5,000) on top of the ongoing AUM fee. We don't. Why? I prefer to demonstrate value on the front end. I want prospective clients to experience the depth of our planning before they make a long-term commitment. The comprehensive plan we build isn't a product we sell separately; it's the foundation of the ongoing relationship.

**We think of retirement income planning as a process, not an event.** Yes, retirement might be an event. You pick a date and stop working. But retirement income planning is a continuous process of adjustment and monitoring as life unfolds. The plan we create in year one will evolve in years two, five, and ten as markets change, tax laws change, your health changes, and your goals change. Our fee structure supports that ongoing process.

**We're product agnostic.** We don't use commission-based products. We don't receive any payments from fund companies or insurance companies. Our only compensation is the fee you pay our firm. This eliminates a layer of potential conflicts.

**We focus on what we can control.** Our philosophy centers on tax optimization, cost minimization through low-cost ETFs, evidence-based asset allocation, and systematic decision-making. We're not trying to beat the market or pick winning stocks. We're trying to optimize the factors that are within our control. This approach isn't driven by what generates fees for us; it's driven by what the research shows actually works.

**We recommend strategies that reduce our fee when appropriate.** If a client should pay off a mortgage, fund long-term care insurance, or make a large gift to children, we'll recommend it even though it reduces the assets we manage (and thus our fee). The relationship only works long-term if we consistently act in your best interest.

Just as I was editing this chapter, a client called to fully distribute an inherited IRA worth about $78,000 so he could gift money to his church. Great idea!

Is our model perfect? No. Every model has conflicts. But we work hard to be transparent about those conflicts and to structure our practice in ways that align our interests with yours.

## Questions to Ask About Compensation

If you're evaluating an advisor (whether your current advisor or a potential new one), here are the questions you should ask:

"**How are you compensated?**" This should get a clear, direct answer. If the advisor is evasive or says "it's complicated," that's a red flag.

"**Do you receive any compensation from product companies, fund companies, or anyone other than me?**" This reveals revenue sharing, 12b-1 fees, trail commissions, or other payments you might not otherwise know about.

"**What conflicts of interest does your compensation model create?**" A good advisor will acknowledge conflicts directly and explain how they manage them. An advisor who claims to have no conflicts is either naive or dishonest.

"**Are you required by law to act in my best interest all of the time?**" Some advisors (particularly those who are dual-registered as both investment advisors and broker-dealer representatives) operate as fiduciaries when providing investment advice but under a different standard when selling products. You want someone who is always on your side.

"**What do I receive for the fee I pay?**" Is it just investment management? Or does it include comprehensive retirement income planning, tax planning, ongoing coordination, and regular reviews?

"**Can you show me an example of a time when you recommended something that reduced your compensation because it was in a client's best interest?**" This is the behavioral test. If they can't give you a specific example, that's concerning.

"**How do you charge for the initial retirement income plan?**" If they charge a large upfront fee before you've experienced their value, ask yourself whether that feels right. If they don't charge separately, ask why and make sure you understand what ongoing fees will be.

## When Fee Structure Reveals Deeper Problems

Sometimes, questions about compensation reveal that you don't actually understand what you're paying for or what service you're receiving. That's a problem regardless of fee structure.

If you can't clearly articulate what value you receive from your advisor, that's worth examining. If you're paying 1% of assets annually but only hear from your advisor once a year with a performance update, that's worth questioning. If you're paying for comprehensive planning but only receiving investment management, that's a mismatch.

The fee structure matters less than whether you're receiving real value for what you're paying and whether your advisor has the expertise to deliver that value.

## The Bottom Line

I started this chapter by saying I don't care much about which fee model an advisor uses. What I care about is transparency, expertise, and consistent behavior in your best interest.

You should care about the same things.

An AUM-based advisor can be excellent if they're transparent, expert, and consistently act as a fiduciary. A commission-based advisor can be excellent under the same conditions. A fee-only advisor can be excellent under the same conditions.

Conversely, any fee structure can hide incompetence or conflicts if the advisor isn't transparent about how they're paid, lacks specialized expertise, or consistently makes recommendations that benefit them more than you.

So ask the questions. Expect clear answers. And evaluate your advisor based on whether they have specialized retirement income expertise, whether they're transparent about compensation and conflicts, and whether their recommendations consistently reflect your best interests.

If your advisor checks all those boxes, the specific fee structure matters less than you might think.

If your advisor fails any of those tests, the fee structure is the least of your problems.

In the next chapter, we'll talk about how to evaluate whether your advisor actually has retirement income expertise. I'll give you specific questions to ask and red flags to watch for that will help you determine whether you're working with a specialist or a generalist advisor applying generic advice to retirement challenges.

## Key Takeaways

- **There is no 'perfect' fee arrangement.** Commission-based advisors might favor higher-cost products. AUM-based advisors might avoid strategies that reduce assets under management. Fee-only advisors might minimize time once fees are collected. What matters more than the model is transparency about conflicts and demonstrated expertise to overcome them.

- **Hidden fees compound the obvious ones.** Many clients know their advisory fee but don't realize they're also paying 1%+ in mutual fund expenses, transaction costs, or embedded annuity charges. Total cost, including both advisory fees and underlying investment expenses, should be clear and justified by the value provided.

- **Expertise matters more than fee structure.** The "cheapest" advisor often costs far more through missed tax planning opportunities and generic withdrawal strategies. A higher fee that includes comprehensive retirement income planning can easily save you 10-20x the fee difference through tax optimization and strategic decisions.

# Chapter 7: Red Flags of a Generalist

*"The beginning of wisdom is found in doubting; by doubting we come to the question, and by seeking we may come upon the truth."*

— Pierre Abelard

Before we get into the specifics of what to look for in a retirement income specialist, I want to address something that stops many people from even starting this evaluation process: they feel awkward about it.

"I don't want to seem like I'm interrogating my advisor," a prospective client told me recently. "It feels rude to ask all these questions about their credentials and approach."

Let me be direct: it's not rude. It's responsible.

You're about to trust someone with managing your financial security for potentially the next 30 years. You're going to pay them tens or hundreds of thousands of dollars in fees. The decisions they help you make, or fail to help you make, could cost or save you hundreds of thousands more.

This is one of the most important professional relationships of your retirement. You have every right to evaluate whether someone is qualified for that responsibility. In fact, you have an obligation to yourself and your family to do so.

Think about it this way: Would you hire a contractor to renovate your home without asking about their experience, seeing examples of their work, checking references, and getting a detailed proposal? Of course not.

Would you hire an attorney to handle a complex legal matter without understanding their specialization, their track record, and their approach to cases like yours? Absolutely not.

So why would you hire, or continue with, a financial advisor without thoroughly evaluating their expertise, understanding their approach, and determining whether they're actually qualified for retirement income planning?

This isn't an interrogation. It's due diligence. And any professional advisor will welcome these questions. In fact, an advisor who gets defensive or dismissive when you ask about their qualifications is telling you something important: they're not confident in their expertise.

The entire purpose of this book is to give you the framework to evaluate retirement advisors with confidence. You now understand the difference between generalists and retirement income planning. You know the dangerous defaults generalist advisors use. You understand the specialized knowledge retirement income planning requires.

Now comes the practical question: How do you actually evaluate whether an advisor has the depth and sophistication required for retirement income planning?

There are two types of red flags to watch for: technical gaps and behavioral patterns. Let me walk you through both.

## How to Use This Chapter

In the previous chapters, we've covered the foundational differences between generalist advisors and retirement income planning. You understand that they're different specialties. You know the dangerous defaults that accumulation advisors often use. You're aware of the compensation structures and conflicts that exist.

Now comes the practical question: How do you actually evaluate whether an advisor has the depth and sophistication required for retirement income planning?

This chapter is about red flags. In the next chapter, we'll cover green lights. But first, I want to show you what lack of sophistication looks like.

I'm going to walk you through scenarios I encounter regularly in my practice. Pay attention to the difference between a simple response and a sophisticated one. The pattern will become clear: advisors who lack retirement income expertise give simple answers to complicated questions, not because they're trying to mislead you, but because they genuinely don't see the complexity.

## PART 1: Technical Skill Red Flags - What They Say Reveals What They Know

The way an advisor responds to complex situations immediately reveals their level of expertise. Generalist advisors tend to give simple, generic answers to complicated questions. Retirement income specialists recognize complexity and ask follow-up questions before making recommendations.

Here are scenarios common for affluent pre-retirees. Pay attention not just to whether the advisor knows the "right answer," but to how they approach the question.

### Scenario 1: Withdrawal Sequencing Across Multiple Account Types

You have money in a traditional IRA, Roth IRA, and taxable accounts. You ask: "Where should I take withdrawals from each year?"

**What a generalist advisor typically says:** "Let's take it proportionally from all accounts to maintain your asset allocation."

**What a retirement income specialist says:** "The optimal sequence depends on several factors specific to you. Generally, we start with taxable accounts because of favorable capital gains rates, then strategically use traditional IRA withdrawals while managing your tax bracket, and preserve Roth the longest since it's tax-free forever. But your specific situation might be different. Are we planning Roth conversions? That changes everything. Are you close to Medicare IRMAA income thresholds? That affects timing. Do you have charitable giving plans? QCDs from your IRA might make sense. What do you want your children to inherit? Roth assets pass tax-free to heirs. Let me show you projections for different sequencing strategies and their tax implications over 20 years."

The difference: One applies a simple rule. The other recognizes your situation is unique and shows you the analysis.

**Scenario 2: The RMD Tax Bomb**

You're 64 with $2 million in traditional IRAs. You ask about retirement planning.

**What a generalist advisor typically says:** "You have plenty saved. At 4%, you can withdraw $80,000 annually. You're in great shape."

**What a retirement income specialist says:** "You have substantial retirement assets, but we need to address a future tax issue. At age 73, you'll be required to start taking minimum distributions from that $2 million IRA. If we don't do anything between now and then, those RMDs will force you to take large taxable distributions, potentially $80,000-$100,000 annually, whether you need the money or not. That could push you into the 24% or 32% tax bracket and trigger Medicare IRMAA surcharges. But you have a nine-year window to do strategic Roth conversions while you're in a lower bracket. Let me model out what converting $75,000-$100,000 annually would look like. We'd pay taxes now at 22-24%, but it dramatically reduces your future RMDs and saves you potentially $150,000+ in lifetime taxes. Let's also coordinate this with your Social Security claiming strategy and any other income sources you'll have."

The difference: One sees adequate assets. The other sees a tax planning opportunity with a limited window.

**Scenario 3: Healthcare Bridge to Medicare**

You're 62 and want to retire before Medicare eligibility at 65.

**What a generalist advisor typically says:** "You'll need to get health insurance for those three years. You can probably get it through the ACA marketplace or COBRA from your employer."

**What a retirement income specialist says:** "Healthcare for ages 62-65 is a critical planning component. Let's model several options and their costs. COBRA from your employer might run $24,000-$30,000 annually for family coverage, and it only lasts 18 months. ACA marketplace coverage could be less expensive, but here's what most people don't realize: your eligibility for premium subsidies depends on your income. If we manage your income strategically during these years, controlling Roth conversions, timing of asset sales, managing distributions, you might qualify for significant subsidies. I've seen clients reduce their healthcare costs from $2,000/month to $400/month by keeping their modified adjusted gross income just below the subsidy cliff. This requires year-by-year income planning, but the savings can be $40,000-$50,000 over three years. We also need to think about whether retiring at 62 versus 63 or 64 changes this calculation, and how healthcare costs affect your overall withdrawal strategy."

The difference: One acknowledges the need. The other shows you how to strategically manage it for substantial savings.

**Scenario 4: Social Security Claiming for High Earners**

You and your spouse both had successful careers. You're wondering when to claim Social Security.

**What a generalist advisor typically says:** "Social Security is a personal decision. Some people take it early, some wait. It's really up to you."

**What a retirement income specialist says:** "For high earners like you, Social Security claiming is one of the most consequential decisions you'll make. Let me show you specific scenarios. If you claim at 62, your benefit might be $2,500/month. If you delay to 70, it grows to $4,400/month because of delayed retirement credits, roughly 76% higher. Over a 25-year retirement, that's a difference of $570,000 in lifetime benefits. But it's more complex than just 'wait longer gets more money.' We need to analyze: What's your health and family longevity? What other income sources do you have to bridge the gap if you delay? How will your benefits be taxed given your other income? What's the survivor benefit impact? if you die first, your spouse gets the higher of your two benefits for life. Are you still working? Benefits claimed before your full retirement age get reduced if you earn above certain thresholds. Let me run a detailed breakeven analysis and coordinate this with your overall tax strategy and withdrawal plan."

The difference: One treats it as a preference. The other treats it as a major financial decision requiring comprehensive analysis.

**Scenario 5: Charitable Giving Strategies**

You tell your advisor you'd like to give $20,000 annually to charity during retirement.

**What a generalist advisor typically says:** "That's great. We can set up automatic distributions to your favorite charities."

**What a retirement income specialist says:** "Charitable giving creates planning opportunities we should optimize. First question: Are you over 70½? If so, qualified charitable distributions directly from your IRA to charity count toward your RMD but don't show up as taxable income. That's often better than taking a distribution, paying tax, then donating and taking a deduction, especially since the higher standard deduction means many retirees don't itemize anymore. If you're not 70½ yet, we should think about timing. Do you have highly appreciated stock in your taxable account? Donating appreciated securities lets you avoid capital gains tax and get a deduction for the full fair market value. Or if you're in a high-income year, bunching multiple years of giving using a donor-advised fund might make sense: get the deduction when your rate is high, then distribute to charities over time. And this affects your overall withdrawal strategy. If you're doing $20,000 in QCDs annually, that's $20,000 less you need from other accounts. Let me show you how different charitable strategies affect your tax situation over the next 10 years."

The difference: One facilitates the gift. The other optimizes the tax efficiency.

**Scenario 6: Concentrated Stock Position**

You have $800,000 of your company's stock in your portfolio from years of employee stock purchase programs.

**What a generalist advisor typically says:** "That's a lot of concentration risk. We should diversify that over time."

**What a retirement income specialist says:** "Having 40% of your portfolio in a single stock creates significant risk, so yes, we need to address it. But how we do it matters for taxes and timing. Let me ask some questions first: What's your cost basis in these shares? If you've held them long-term and have low basis, selling creates a large capital gains tax bill. Are you still working? If you're about to retire and will have lower income years, maybe we spread the sales across those years to stay in the 15% capital gains bracket instead of 20%. Do you have charitable intent? Donating some of the appreciated shares to charity avoids the capital gains entirely. Are you holding any shares that have lost value? We can tax-loss harvest those against gains elsewhere. Also, let's coordinate this with your Roth conversion strategy. We don't want to create a year where we're recognizing large capital gains and doing Roth conversions simultaneously, spiking your income. I'll model out a multi-year diversification strategy that minimizes tax impact while reducing your risk exposure systematically."

The difference: One identifies the problem. The other creates a tax-efficient solution.

**Scenario 7: Deferred Compensation Complexity**

You have $600,000 in deferred compensation that will pay out over five years starting when you retire.

**What a generalist advisor typically says:** "Great, that'll provide additional income during your early retirement years."

**What a retirement income specialist says:** "Deferred compensation changes your entire income planning strategy. For the next five years, you'll have substantial W-2 income from the deferrals. That means: You'll be in a higher tax bracket during those years, which limits Roth conversion opportunities. Your Social Security benefits, if you claim them, will be taxed at a higher rate. You might hit Medicare

IRMAA thresholds, increasing your premiums. You'll need less from your portfolio during this period. So we need to plan in two distinct phases. Years 1-5 while deferred comp is paying: minimize portfolio withdrawals, be careful about Roth conversions, and possibly delay Social Security claiming. Years 6+ after deferred comp ends: you'll have a big drop in income, which creates opportunities for larger Roth conversions, potentially a good time to start Social Security, and we'll need more from your portfolio to maintain your lifestyle. We also need to know: is this deferred comp portable if you want to move states? Some plans allow it, some don't. That affects your timing if you're considering relocating. Let me build a comprehensive plan that accounts for both phases."

The difference: One sees additional income. The other sees how it affects every other planning decision.

**Scenario 8: Moving from Wisconsin to Florida**

You mention you're thinking about moving to Florida when you retire.

**What a generalist advisor typically says:** "Florida has great weather and no state income tax. That'll save you money."

**What a retirement income specialist says:** "A move to Florida has significant financial planning implications we need to coordinate carefully. Timing is critical. Wisconsin will scrutinize your residency change. They don't want to lose the tax revenue from your retirement account distributions. We need to establish clear Florida domicile: get Florida driver's license, register to vote there, change your legal address, and spend more than 183 days there annually. But here's where it gets complex: When do you move relative to your retirement date? If you have deferred compensation or RSUs vesting, is that Wisconsin-source income even after you move? What about your IRA distributions: do those become Florida income only after you establish residency, or does Wisconsin try to claim them? If you're selling your Wisconsin home, are you doing that before or after establishing Florida residency? The timing affects capital gains treatment. And Florida has no state income tax, but it also has no state income tax deduction for large charitable gifts: does that change your giving strategy? Also, think about estate planning: Florida and Wisconsin have different rules. We should review your estate documents with an attorney familiar with Florida law. Let me connect you with a tax attorney who specializes in multi-state residency issues, so we plan this transition properly and avoid unexpected tax bills."

The difference: One acknowledges the benefit. The other sees the complexity and helps you navigate it without mistakes.

### What These Scenarios Reveal

Notice the pattern? Generalist advisors give quick, simple answers. Retirement income specialists immediately see the complexity, ask clarifying questions, and show you the analysis.

This isn't about memorizing the "right" answer to these scenarios. It's about recognizing whether your advisor has the depth to handle sophisticated planning.

If you ask these kinds of questions and get simple reassurance rather than detailed analysis, that's a red flag. Not because the advisor is wrong. Sometimes the simple answer is fine. But because they're not demonstrating the specialized knowledge required for comprehensive retirement income planning.

## PART 2: Behavioral Red Flags - How They Make You Feel Matters

Technical competence is necessary but not sufficient. You also need to pay attention to how interactions with your advisor feel. These behavioral patterns often emerge gradually and signal deeper issues.

**Red Flag #1: This Doesn't Feel Personal Anymore**

This is usually the first crack in a long-standing relationship.

The meetings start feeling recycled. Your advisor is saying things you've heard before. The advice sounds familiar before they finish the sentence. They're talking *at* you, not *with* you, delivering information rather than having a conversation.

Most telling: your situation changes, but their recommendations don't evolve.

Example: A couple I know had been with their advisor for 18 years. At 60, they mentioned they were thinking about retiring at 62 instead of 65 because of some health concerns. Their advisor adjusted the retirement age in his software and said, "Looks like you're still fine. We'll just need to be a little more conservative with spending."

No discussion of healthcare costs for the three years before Medicare. No analysis of whether retiring earlier changes Social Security timing. No conversation about whether their health concerns affect longevity assumptions or long-term care planning. Just a software adjustment.

That's when they realized: we're not getting personalized advice anymore. We're getting template updates.

This isn't necessarily incompetence. Sometimes it's simply a capacity restraint. The advisor has taken on too many clients and can't give everyone the attention they need. Sometimes it's complacency in a long relationship. Sometimes it's that the advisor's skills matched your needs during accumulation, but don't match retirement complexity.

Whatever the cause, when planning stops feeling customized to you, that's a signal.

**Red Flag #2: Big Decisions Start Getting Hand-Waved**

People tolerate vague advice for small things. They don't tolerate it for decisions that matter.

This red flag shows up when you ask about something significant, like Social Security claiming, pension elections, retirement timing, major tax decisions, and get quick, confident answers without much analysis.

"Take the lump sum, we can invest it."

"Most people claim Social Security at full retirement age."

"You should be fine."

What causes doubt isn't necessarily that the answer is wrong. It's how quickly the answer comes.

A colleague told me about asking his advisor whether he should take his pension as $85,000 annually for life or a $1.3 million lump sum. The advisor spent maybe 30 seconds saying, "Take the lump sum. We'll manage it, and you'll have more flexibility."

No questions about his health. No discussion of his wife's situation or survivor benefits. No analysis of whether they needed a guaranteed income to cover baseline expenses. No evaluation of the pension's cost-of-living adjustments. No consideration of the pension plan's financial health.

Just an instant recommendation.

That's when my colleague thought, "This actually matters. Maybe I should talk to someone who'll analyze it more carefully."

Retirement income specialists don't give instant answers to complex questions. They ask follow-up questions, show you the analysis, and walk through trade-offs. When an advisor hand-waves major decisions, they're revealing they haven't thought deeply about your specific situation.

### Red Flag #3: I Don't Know What Happens If Things Go Wrong

This is psychologically huge. Clients rarely expect perfect outcomes. But they do expect their advisor to have thought about what happens if things don't go as planned.

The red flag: no discussion of downside scenarios. No explanation of what would trigger changes to the strategy. No guardrails or thresholds.

Example: A prospective client showed me his retirement plan from his previous advisor. Beautiful charts showing his portfolio growing smoothly over 30 years. 89% probability of success based on historical returns.

I asked, "What happens if we get another 2008-style market crash in your second year of retirement? What changes?"

He had no idea. His advisor had never discussed it.

"What if inflation runs higher than the 3% assumption for several years?"

No idea.

"At what point would you adjust spending? What's the trigger?"

His advisor had never mentioned triggers.

The plan felt like a black box. Projections going in, probability percentage coming out, no insight into what happens if reality differs from assumptions.

Other clients experience the opposite problem: the plan feels like a single straight line forever. Same withdrawal amount every year, same allocation, same strategy, regardless of what happens in markets or their lives.

Both extremes create the same unease: "I don't think we've actually thought this through."

Retirement income specialists build contingency thinking into plans. They discuss what changes at different portfolio values, what spending adjustments might be needed if returns disappoint, what strategies shift if health or family situations change. The plan has flexibility built in, not rigid assumptions.

**Red Flag #4: The Advisor Sounds Certain, But I Feel Uneasy**

This is subtle but powerful. Confidence without nuance erodes trust over time.

It shows up as overuse of reassurance language:

- "You don't need to worry about that."
- "This is what everyone does."
- "Trust me, you'll be fine."

Or dismissal of "what if" questions:

- "That's not going to happen."
- "You're overthinking this."
- "Let's not complicate things unnecessarily."

Or framing your concerns as anxiety rather than prudence:

- "You're worried about things that aren't worth worrying about."
- "The markets always recover. You just need to relax."

Here's what happens: you start saying to yourself, "He's probably right, but..."

That "but" is the moment. You're no longer fully confident in the advice, even though you can't articulate exactly why.

Retirement income specialists are comfortable with nuance. They'll say things like:

- "There's no perfect answer here. Let's talk through the trade-offs."

- "This strategy works well if X happens, but if Y happens, we'd need to adjust."
- "That's a reasonable concern. Here's how we account for it."

They don't need to project absolute certainty because they've built flexibility into the plan. They're comfortable discussing what they don't know and how they handle uncertainty.

When an advisor consistently projects certainty about inherently uncertain things, be wary. Either they don't understand the complexity, or they're uncomfortable acknowledging what they don't know.

**Red Flag #5: The Conversation Feels Defensive**

This is often the point of no return emotionally.

It happens when you ask reasonable questions about credentials, about alternative strategies, about second opinions, about how something works, and the response is dismissive, irritated, or minimizing.

- "Are you questioning my recommendations?"
- "I've been doing this for 25 years. I think I know what I'm doing."
- "If you want to work with someone else, that's your choice."

- "Those other strategies don't really work for most people."

Not all pushback is defensiveness. Sometimes advisors appropriately push back on ideas that don't make sense for your situation. Healthy professional relationships include disagreement and honest feedback.

The difference is tone and openness. A retirement income specialist might say:

- "That's an interesting idea. Let me explain why I don't think it's best for you, but I'm happy to run the numbers if you'd like to see it."
- "I'm not familiar with that strategy. Let me research it and we can discuss it next time."
- "I understand why you're asking about credentials. Let me walk you through my training in retirement income planning."

When you ask questions and feel like you're being shut down rather than engaged with, you stop asking questions. That's when you emotionally disengage from the relationship.

You're not leaving because you want to. You're leaving because you no longer feel safe being curious or concerned.

### Red Flag #6: I'm Staying Out of Loyalty, Not Judgment

This is where many people finally give themselves permission to make a change.

They realize:

- "We've stayed because it would feel awkward to leave."
- "We're loyal to the person who helped us accumulate wealth."
- "But this phase feels different. Our needs have changed."

This connects back to everything we discussed in Chapter 3 about when loyalty becomes a liability.

The advisor who was excellent at helping you build wealth over 20 years might not have the specialized training for retirement income planning. That's not a character flaw. It's not even a competency problem in their domain. It's a mismatch between what you need now and what they're equipped to provide.

Recognizing this isn't disloyal. It's honest.

You can be grateful for what your advisor did during accumulation while acknowledging they're not the right fit for retirement. You can appreciate the relationship while recognizing you need different expertise now.

The red flag isn't that you're questioning the relationship. The red flag is when you realize you're staying out of obligation rather than conviction. When you're avoiding the evaluation because you don't want to hurt feelings, not because you're confident in the expertise.

That's the moment many people finally decide: "I need to at least talk to a retirement income specialist and see the difference."

## Moving Forward

These red flags, both technical and behavioral, aren't meant to make you paranoid about your current advisor. They're meant to help you honestly evaluate whether you have the specialized expertise you need for this phase.

Some of you will go through this list and think, "Actually, my advisor is pretty sophisticated. They do this kind of analysis." Excellent. You might already be working with someone who has retirement income expertise even if they don't explicitly market themselves that way.

Others will recognize multiple red flags and realize, "I don't think we're getting the depth of planning we need."

In the next chapter, we'll talk about what to look for in a retirement income specialist: the credentials that matter, the questions to ask, the process to expect, and how to evaluate whether someone actually has the expertise to handle your retirement planning.

Because identifying red flags is only useful if you know what green lights look like.

## Key Takeaways:

- **Simple answers to complex questions reveal knowledge gaps.** When you mention RSUs, deferred compensation, pension decisions, or multi-state moves, a specialist immediately asks detailed follow-up questions. A generalist gives quick, confident answers without recognizing the layers of complexity. The sophistication shows in what questions they ask, not what answers they provide.

- **Behavioral red flags matter as much as technical gaps**. If meetings feel recycled, if big decisions get hand-waved, if you don't know what happens when things go wrong, if your advisor sounds certain but you feel uneasy, or if questions about credentials trigger defensiveness, these patterns reveal deeper issues than any single technical mistake.

- **You're staying out of inertia, not conviction.** The moment you realize you're continuing the relationship out of loyalty, guilt, or avoiding awkwardness rather than confidence in their specialized expertise is the moment to at least explore alternatives. You're not being disloyal; you're being responsible about one of your most important professional relationships.

# Chapter 8: Green Lights - Recognizing True Retirement Income Expertise

*"When someone shows you who they are, believe them the first time."*

— Maya Angelou

In the last chapter, we looked at red flags. Simple answers to complex questions. Generic advice that ignores your specific situation. Missing the multiple layers of retirement income planning because they've never studied it systematically.

Now let me show you what true retirement income expertise looks like. These are the green lights, the signals that tell you someone has invested in developing specialized knowledge and has the sophistication to handle your complex situation.

Here's what you need to understand: not every advisor needs to be a retirement income specialist. Generalist and accumulation-oriented advisors serve an important role. They help people build wealth during their working years. That's valuable work, and many do it well.

But if you're approaching or in retirement, you need someone who has gone deeper. Someone who has studied the specialized domains of retirement income planning. Someone who sees complexity where others see simplicity.

Let me show you what that looks like.

## The Two Dimensions of Retirement Income Expertise

Before I walk you through the specific green lights, I need to address something most people don't realize: the best retirement income specialists operate on two levels simultaneously.

The first level is what we've been discussing throughout this book: the technical financial planning expertise. Tax-efficient withdrawal strategies, Social Security optimization, healthcare planning, multi-year tax projections. This is the quantitative, analytical side of retirement income planning.

But there's a second level that's equally important and often overlooked: the life planning side of retirement.

When I developed the curriculum for the RICP® program at The American College of Financial Services, I created an entire unit called "The Psychology of Retirement" because I recognized something critical: all the brilliant tax planning in the world doesn't matter if someone retires and discovers they have no sense of purpose, their marriage is strained because they haven't aligned on what retirement looks like, or they're isolated because they moved somewhere without building a social network.

Remember the story I shared in Chapter 4 about my parents spending their first few years of retirement figuring out where to live? Multiple moves, hundreds of thousands in transaction costs, precious "go-go years" spent in trial and error? That wasn't a financial planning failure. That was a life planning gap that had massive financial consequences.

The non-financial aspects of retirement often pose bigger risks than the financial ones, especially for affluent clients who have their basic financial security covered. Questions like:

What will give you purpose and meaning when your career identity is gone?

Have you and your spouse actually discussed what you each want retirement to look like?

Where do you want to be geographically, and is that based on fantasy or actual experience living there?

How will you build and maintain social connections as you age?

What's your relationship with health, wellness, and staying physically active?

How do you want to spend your time when you have 2,000+ hours a year that were previously consumed by work?

These aren't soft, touchy-feely extras. These are core components of successful retirement that directly impact your financial decisions: where you'll live affects your budget and tax situation, your activity level affects healthcare costs, and your social connections affect whether you'll really want to travel or prefer to stay closer to family.

A comprehensive retirement income specialist addresses both dimensions. They're sophisticated on the technical financial side, and they help you think through the life transition side. They ask about your vision for retirement, not just your spending assumptions. They probe whether you've really thought through housing decisions, not just whether you can afford them. They encourage you to discuss expectations with your spouse before retirement, not after you discover you have conflicting visions.

This dual expertise is what separates truly comprehensive retirement income planning from simple portfolio management with some tax optimization layered on top.

As you evaluate advisors using the green lights I'm about to share, pay attention to both dimensions. Do they only talk about money? Or do they also ask about purpose, relationships, housing, health, and how you'll actually structure your days?

The best specialists recognize that retirement is a life transition, not just a financial transaction.

Now, let's look at the specific signals that indicate someone has this depth of expertise.

## Green Light 1: They Lead with Planning, Not Products

In initial conversations, a retirement income specialist asks detailed questions about your situation, your goals, your concerns, and your flexibility. They want to understand your complete picture before making any recommendations.

They're not leading with "here's our portfolio approach" or "we use this investment strategy for all our retirement clients." They're asking questions and listening.

When I meet with prospective clients, I spend the first meeting almost entirely on discovery. What does your ideal retirement look like? What are your biggest concerns? What keeps you up at night financially? What are your priorities for legacy, for family, for lifestyle? What have the past experiences with financial planners been like, and what are you looking for?

Only after understanding your situation do we start talking about strategies and approaches. The planning drives the implementation, not the other way around.

If an advisor is pitching you their standard approach before they've thoroughly understood your situation, that's a problem. They're trying to fit you into their template rather than building a plan around your needs.

## Green Light 2: They Can Walk You Through a Systematic Process

When you ask, "What's your process for retirement income planning?" they should be able to articulate clear steps. Discovery, analysis, strategy development, plan presentation, implementation, and ongoing management. They've done this many times and have a refined approach.

I can walk a prospective client through exactly what the first 90 days look like, what deliverables they'll receive, and how we'll work together on an ongoing basis. Discovery meetings to understand your situation. Comprehensive analysis of your income sources, tax situation, and planning needs. Strategy development that addresses your specific circumstances. Plan presentation where we walk through everything in detail. Implementation with clear action steps. Ongoing review and optimization.

If your advisor can't articulate their process clearly, they might not have one. Or they might be making it up as they go, which isn't what you want for something this important.

A systematic process doesn't mean rigid or inflexible. It means they've thought through how to serve clients comprehensively and consistently. They're not reinventing the wheel with each new client.

## Green Light 3: They Immediately Recognize Complexity

This is the pattern you saw throughout the scenarios in the last chapter. When you mention anything complex (deferred comp, concentrated stock, pension decision, multi-state move, healthcare bridge), their first response isn't a quick answer. It's more questions.

"Tell me about the vesting schedule." "Where is that stock held?" "Let me see your pension's Summary Plan Description." "When are you moving relative to your retirement date?" "What's your cost basis in that concentrated position?"

They're probing for the details that matter because they know these situations have multiple layers. They've seen enough complex situations to know that simple questions rarely have simple answers when the stakes are this high.

If an advisor gives you a quick, confident answer to a complex question without asking follow-up questions, be skeptical. Either they don't see the complexity, or they're oversimplifying to sound confident.

## Green Light 4: They Can Articulate Multiple Dimensions

Listen to how they explain their thinking. A retirement income specialist will say things like: "When we analyze your pension decision, we're evaluating longevity risk, interest rate environment, survivor benefits, cost-of-living adjustments, your income floor needs, tax implications, and your risk capacity for managing investments."

They're not just saying "we'll run some numbers." They're articulating the framework they use to think through complex decisions.

Or they might say: "When we coordinate your Social Security claiming with your Roth conversion strategy, we need to model out your tax brackets year by year, understand Medicare IRMAA thresholds, consider survivor benefits, and look at your overall income sustainability."

That multi-dimensional thinking comes from specialized training. Which brings me to an important point.

The knowledge I'm describing isn't something advisors pick up through general experience. It requires dedicated study.

The RICP designation I teach at The American College is three intensive courses covering retirement income processes, sources of retirement income (Social Security, pensions, business income, investments), and managing the retirement plan (taxes, healthcare, housing, estate).

When I teach advisors pursuing this designation, they're often surprised by how much depth is required. It's not a weekend course. It's months of study covering executive compensation strategies, pension analysis, multi-state tax issues, healthcare coordination, long-term care funding, and estate planning integration.

One advisor told me after completing the program: "I've been advising retirees for fifteen years. I thought I knew this stuff. I didn't realize how much I didn't know."

If your advisor has invested in this level of specialized training, whether through RICP or equivalent depth of education, that's a strong signal that they take retirement income planning seriously. They've recognized the gaps in their knowledge and done something about it.

## Green Light 5: They Use Specialized Tools

A retirement income specialist has purpose-built software and can show you examples. Multi-year tax projection software that models Roth conversions across different scenarios. Pension analysis tools that show breakeven points under different longevity assumptions. Social Security optimization software that evaluates spousal coordination and survivor benefits.

These aren't generic financial planning tools. They're specialized for retirement income analysis.

When you ask, "Can you show me how you analyze this?" they should be able to pull up examples. Obviously, not other clients' actual data, but demonstrations of their analytical approach.

In my practice, I can show you what a multi-year tax projection looks like. I can demonstrate our Social Security analysis tool. I can walk you through how we model different withdrawal sequences. These tools exist because retirement income planning requires specific types of analysis that go beyond what general planning software provides.

If an advisor is using only generic planning software with simple projections, they're not doing the sophisticated analysis your situation requires.

## Green Light 6: They Talk About Coordination

Retirement income planning requires working with other professionals. A specialist will say things like:

"We should have a joint meeting with your CPA before year-end to coordinate Roth conversions and estimated tax payments."

"Have you updated your estate plan since your net worth increased? Let's get your attorney involved in this conversation."

"For your multi-state move, I'd recommend bringing in a tax attorney who specializes in residency issues."

They're not trying to do everything themselves. They recognize when specialized expertise is needed and they coordinate effectively.

In my practice, I work regularly with CPAs, estate planning attorneys, and other specialists. I'm not threatened by bringing them in. I welcome it because I want the best outcome for my clients. I know my expertise, and I know when someone else's expertise is needed.

An advisor who tries to do everything themselves, who dismisses the need for other professionals, or who gets territorial about "their" client is probably not operating at a sophisticated level. Complex situations require a team approach.

## Green Light 7: They Proactively Identify Issues

A retirement income specialist doesn't wait for you to ask about every potential issue. They surface things you haven't considered.

"You mentioned retiring at 62. Have you thought about health insurance until Medicare at 65? This affects your withdrawal strategy significantly."

"You're planning to move to Florida. When relative to your retirement date? If you have deferred compensation, we need to think about state tax sourcing."

"I see you're considering claiming Social Security at 67. Before we finalize that, let's make sure we've looked at survivor benefits for your spouse and how this integrates with your other income sources."

"You have a large traditional IRA and you're retiring now. Have we talked about the Roth conversion opportunity in the years before RMDs begin?"

They're thinking several moves ahead, connecting decisions that might seem separate. They see how different pieces of your financial life interact.

This kind of proactive planning comes from experience with complex situations and from having a systematic framework for thinking through retirement income. They know what questions to ask because they've asked them many times before.

## Green Light 8: They're Transparent About Costs and Conflicts

They voluntarily explain how they're compensated, what conflicts that creates, and how they manage those conflicts. They're upfront about total costs, including both advisory fees and underlying fund expenses.

They don't wait for you to ask. They proactively address it because they know it matters to you and because they have nothing to hide.

In my first meeting with prospective clients, I explain our fee structure, how we're compensated, and what potential conflicts exist with an AUM-based model. I'm clear about what services that fee includes. I explain our investment philosophy and why we focus on low-cost ETFs rather than active management or commission products.

An advisor who is evasive about fees, who makes you pull information out of them, or who gets defensive when you ask about costs is sending a signal. Either they're not confident in their value proposition, or they're not comfortable with the transparency that characterizes professional relationships.

## Green Light 9: They Have Focus and Appropriate Minimums

Here's something that might surprise you: having account minimums is actually a positive signal for specialization.

At Stockbridge Private Wealth Management, we work primarily with clients who have $1 million or more in investable assets. Not because smaller portfolios don't deserve good planning, but because we've built our practice specifically for the complexity that comes with larger portfolios and the planning needs of successful professionals approaching retirement.

When an advisor serves everyone from $5,000 accounts to $5 million accounts, they can't truly specialize. How much time can they devote to your complex tax planning or multi-year optimization if they're serving 300 clients across a massive range of situations?

Think about it this way: Would you rather work with a surgeon who does twenty different procedures, or one who specializes in the specific procedure you need and has done it hundreds of times?

Specialization means focus. Focus means selectivity about clientele. That's a feature, not a bug.

When an advisor has no minimums and serves everyone, ask yourself: How specialized can they really be? How much individualized attention can you expect?

Now, this doesn't mean higher minimums are always better. It means appropriate minimums for their specialization. An advisor who focuses on young professionals might have a $250,000 minimum. An advisor who specializes in retirement income for affluent clients might have a $1 million or $2 million minimum. The key is that they've defined who they serve best.

## Green Light 10: They Demonstrate Value Upfront

Pay attention to how they structure initial engagement. Are they willing to show you the depth of their planning before asking for a long-term commitment?

At my firm, we don't charge separately for the initial comprehensive retirement income plan. Why? Because I want prospective clients to experience the depth of our planning before they decide whether to work with us long-term.

I want you to see the Social Security analysis, the tax projections, the withdrawal strategy, and how we coordinate all the pieces. Then you can make an informed decision about whether this is the level of planning you want.

Some advisors charge anywhere from $3,000 to $20,000 for an upfront plan before you've experienced their value. That model works for some people. I prefer to demonstrate value first. I'm confident enough in what we do that I'm willing to show it to you before asking for a commitment.

Look for an advisor who is confident enough in their expertise that they're willing to demonstrate it rather than just talk about it.

## Green Light 11: They Welcome Your Questions

When you ask about their approach, their credentials, their process, they're enthusiastic about explaining. They see it as an opportunity to demonstrate expertise, not as a challenge to their authority.

They might even say, "I'm glad you're asking these questions. You should be evaluating whether I'm the right fit for you."

They're not defensive. They're not evasive. They're direct and detailed in their answers because they're confident in what they know and what they do.

An advisor who gets defensive or dismissive when you ask about qualifications is telling you something important: they're not confident in their expertise. Confident specialists welcome scrutiny.

## Green Light 12: They Stay Current

Ask them about continuing education and research. A retirement income specialist will say things like:

"I just attended the Horizons Retirement Conference where research was presented on dynamic withdrawal strategies..."

"Recent work by David Blanchett suggests that..."

"The new SECURE Act 2.0 provisions change how we think about..."

"I'm teaching a session at the FPA conference next month on..."

They're not just relying on "I've been doing this for 25 years." They're actively engaged with evolving research and best practices in retirement income planning.

The field evolves. Tax laws change. Research emerges. Best practices develop. An advisor who isn't staying current isn't serving you as well as they could be.

## Questions to Ask

Let me give you specific questions relevant to the situations we discussed in the last chapter. You don't need to ask all of these, but pick the ones that apply to your situation.

**For everyone:**

- "What percentage of your clients are in retirement or within five years of retirement?"
- "Walk me through your process for creating a comprehensive retirement income plan."
- "How do you coordinate with CPAs and estate planning attorneys?"
- "What specialized training do you have in retirement income planning?"
- "How do you stay current with research and best practices in retirement income?"

**If you have significant traditional IRA balances:**

- "How do you approach Roth conversion planning in the years before RMDs begin?"
- "Can you show me an example of a multi-year tax projection?"
- "How do you coordinate Roth conversions with Social Security timing?"

**If you're retiring before 65:**

- "How do you help clients manage healthcare costs in the Medicare gap?"

- "Can you model ACA coverage with different income scenarios?"
- "What strategies do you use to optimize income for ACA subsidies?"

**If you're a high earner with significant Social Security benefits:**

- "How do you approach Social Security claiming for affluent couples?"
- "Can you show me analysis of how Social Security taxation and Medicare premiums affect the claiming decision?"
- "How do you coordinate Social Security with Roth conversions and other income planning?"

**If you're charitably inclined:**

- "How do you integrate charitable giving into retirement tax planning?"
- "Can you explain qualified charitable distributions and other tax-efficient giving strategies?"
- "How do you coordinate charitable giving with Roth conversions and income management?"

**If you have concentrated stock positions:**

- "How do you approach diversifying concentrated positions tax-efficiently?"

- "Are you familiar with NUA strategies for company stock in 401(k)s?"
- "How do you coordinate diversification with overall tax planning?"

**If you have deferred compensation:**

- "How do you handle retirement planning for clients with deferred compensation?"
- "Can you model how deferred comp affects Social Security timing and Roth conversions?"
- "How do you plan differently for the years with deferred comp versus after it ends?"

**If you're moving to a different state:**

- "What's your experience with multi-state tax planning?"
- "What specialists do you work with for establishing residency?"
- "How do you coordinate state moves with retirement timing and income planning?"

Pay attention not just to whether they can answer these questions, but how they answer them. Do they demonstrate depth? Do they ask you clarifying questions? Do they connect the issue to other aspects of your planning?

## Making the Switch Is Normal

Let me tell you what I see in my practice. The most successful retirees, the ones who have the most confidence and peace of mind, are the ones who treated this transition the same way they treated other major life transitions: by seeking specialized expertise.

They didn't feel guilty about it. They didn't apologize for it. They recognized that their needs had changed, and they found someone whose expertise matched those needs.

I had a client, a retiring orthopedic surgeon, come to me last year from a "Big Bank" advisor he'd worked with for 18 years. He felt awkward about making the change. "My advisor is a good guy," he told me. "He helped me build this portfolio from almost nothing."

Here's what I told him, and what I want you to hear: Your accumulation advisor got you here. That's valuable. That matters. You should be grateful for that.

But getting you here and keeping you here requires different expertise.

He told me, "The pediatrician for my grandkids isn't the one doing knee replacements at my clinic."

Exactly.

Most good accumulation advisors recognize this. They know they're not retirement income specialists. Some actively refer clients out when they approach retirement. Others continue serving those clients but acknowledge they're applying general knowledge to a specialized phase.

The advisors who get defensive when clients ask about retirement income expertise are usually the ones who don't have it. The advisors who are confident in their capabilities either demonstrate specialized training or acknowledge the gap honestly.

You know what's interesting? When I talk to the accumulation advisors whose clients have come to me, they're almost always gracious about it. They understand. Many of them say "I'm glad my client found someone who specializes in this. I want what's best for them."

That's the mature, professional response. If your advisor responds differently, that tells you something about their priorities and their confidence in their own expertise.

## What Successful People Do

I'll tell you another pattern I see. Successful people, the kind of people who built $1 million or $2 million or $5 million portfolios through their careers, didn't get there by being passive. They made active, informed decisions. They sought expertise when they needed it. They weren't afraid to make changes when circumstances warranted it.

Those same instincts that served you well in your career serve you well in retirement. You recognize when you need specialized help. You do your due diligence. You ask questions. You evaluate options. You make informed decisions.

That's not being difficult. That's being responsible. That's being smart. That's using the same judgment that helped you succeed in the first place.

The people who struggle most in retirement, from what I've seen, are often the ones who became passive. Who stayed with advisors out of inertia rather than evaluation. Who didn't ask hard questions because they didn't want to rock the boat.

You didn't build wealth by being passive. Don't transition to retirement that way either.

## Remember

Here's what I want you to remember from these last two chapters: You're not looking for someone who gives you quick, simple answers. You're looking for someone who immediately recognizes complexity, asks probing questions, articulates multiple dimensions of decisions, coordinates with other professionals, demonstrates specialized training, and addresses both the financial and life planning aspects of retirement.

If your current advisor meets that standard, excellent. You're in good hands. Thank them for investing in that expertise and continue working together.

If they don't, it's time to find someone who does.

Not because your current advisor is a bad person or because they've done something wrong. Simply because your needs have changed and you need different expertise.

There's no shame in that.

There's no betrayal in that.

It's just professional specialization working the way it should.

In the next chapter, I'll share something personal. A moment that changed my career and taught me about transitions. Because recognizing you need specialized expertise is one thing, and actually making the change is another.

That final step isn't technical. It's psychological. And it's what we'll explore next.

Want a practical tool to help you evaluate advisors? I've created a free companion guide called *The Retirement Specialist Selection Checklist* with step-by-step guidance for finding qualified specialists, verifying credentials and backgrounds, and all the questions from this chapter organized by category.

https://stockbridgewealth.com/book/

or use this QR code:

**Key Takeaways:**

- **Specialists lead with planning, not products.** The first meeting is almost entirely discovery, understanding your goals, concerns, family situation, and complete financial picture before discussing strategies. They have systematic processes they can clearly articulate, not ad-hoc approaches that vary by client. Implementation follows planning, not the other way around.

- **True expertise shows in how they handle complexity.** When you mention concentrated stock, deferred compensation, business ownership, or multi-state moves, they don't give instant answers. They ask probing questions, identify considerations you haven't thought about, and coordinate with other professionals because they recognize when specialized expertise beyond their own is needed.

- **They demonstrate value before asking for long-term commitment.** Confident specialists show you the depth of their planning upfront rather than charging large fees before you experience their value. They use sophisticated tools, stay current with research and continuing education, and can cite specific examples of proactive strategies rather than just reactive portfolio management.

# Chapter 9: Taking Action

*"The secret of change is to focus all of your energy not on fighting the old, but on building the new."*

— Socrates (attributed)

I was 14 when I decided I wanted to be an airline pilot.

Not "thought it might be cool" or "was interested in." I knew what I wanted to do like it was a calling.

I pestered my parents relentlessly. If I got good grades in my junior year, would they support this? They agreed, probably assuming I'd forget. Well, I didn't. The summer before my senior year of high school, I drove to the local flight school in Madison and booked myself a discovery flight. By the time I graduated high school, I had my private pilot certificate.

The next decade I continued that single-minded focus. Embry-Riddle Aeronautical University. Airline internship. Every odd flying job I could find to build hours: dropping skydivers, towing banners over beaches, hauling cargo through mountain passes in the Rockies. Each job was a stepping stone toward the only goal that mattered.

At 23, I got hired by a regional airline. I'd made it.

Late summer 2005, I was in my hotel room in Rochester, Minnesota, looking forward to three days off when my phone rang. Crew scheduling.

They were organizing a relief flight to New Orleans. Hurricane Katrina had just devastated the Gulf Coast. They had a captain and flight attendants. They needed a first officer. Was I willing?

I didn't hesitate.

The next morning at O'Hare, I met the crew. The airline had loaded everything we could fit: water, medical supplies, and toiletries. But also people. Dam experts from the Army Corps of Engineers. Nurses. Doctors. Specialists with expertise that the region desperately needed.

We couldn't land in New Orleans. The airport was too damaged. Baton Rouge was the closest option, but its runway was compromised. The last third was unusable, which meant we'd be landing on a shortened runway with no margin for error.

The region needed all available fuel, so we had to carry enough for the round trip. If we missed the landing and had to go around, we'd need to divert somewhere else to refuel. There would be no second attempt.

The captain and I flipped a coin for who'd fly which leg.

I won the leg flying into Baton Rouge.

I'd landed thousands of times by that point in my career. But this was different. Shortened runway. Damaged surface. One chance. A plane full of relief workers and supplies. A region in crisis, counting on us to get there. Not to mention the countless people waiting on us to arrive so they could get out.

I remember the approach. The concentration required to hit the touchdown zone perfectly. Not too long, not too short. The relief when the wheels touched exactly where they needed to.

We made it.

On the return flight, we carried survivors. The flight attendants talked with them while I flew. Later, they shared some of the stories. Most of these people had no real plan. They'd stay with family. See what happened. Figure it out as they went.

When we landed back at O'Hare and I got back to my car, something started to shift inside me.

I spent my three-hour drive home to Madison trying to decompress and make sense of it all. All those years of training. The hours of building experience. The sacrifice. The singular focus on becoming an airline pilot. It felt like everything had been building toward that one flight.

And now it was done.

I didn't want to stop flying because I was burned out or disappointed. I'd achieved exactly what I set out to do. But on that long drive home, I knew with absolute certainty that this chapter was over. It was time to do something else.

I’ve since noticed that most major life transitions follow a similar pattern: awareness, then intention, preparation, when the right opportunity presents itself, action. That drive home was my awareness moment.

Eighteen months later, I started working as a financial advisor.

I've thought about that moment many times over the years, but I've rarely shared it outside my family. That unexplainable sense of knowing a transition was complete and something new needed to begin.

I've heard hundreds of clients describe something similar as they approach retirement.

"How did you know it was time to retire?" your friends ask.

Sometimes, health makes the decision. But often, people say something like: "It just felt right." Or "I knew I was done." The career that defined them for decades suddenly felt complete. Not because they hated it or couldn't do it anymore. But because that chapter was finished.

If you're feeling that, trust it. Those instincts are real.

But here's what I learned from my own transition: recognizing it's time to change is only the first step. Understanding what the new phase requires is what determines whether the transition goes well or poorly.

The drive home was my awareness moment. But the next 18 months weren't just about changing careers. They were about understanding what financial advising demanded and preparing myself for it.

The same applies to your retirement transition. Recognizing it's time is step one. Understanding what retirement demands, both financially and psychologically, is step two.

That's where most people get stuck.

## The Hardest Part Isn't the Math

Here's the paradox I see regularly: the people who were best at saving for retirement often struggle most when it's time to spend. The discipline that got you here becomes the barrier to enjoying what you built. You spent 40 years living below your means. Maximizing contributions. Delaying gratification. Every spending decision filtered through "should we really buy this, or could we save it?"

That mindset was correct for accumulation. It got you to $1 million or $2 million or more. You won at saving. But now the rules have changed. But nobody told you. I might not know you personally, but I'm guessing the goal was never to maximize your account balance. The goal was to fund a retirement where you could finally do the things you worked so hard for.

I've watched clients who saved brilliantly and planned carefully struggle to give themselves permission to actually use the money.

The 72-year-old who keeps saying "maybe next year" for that Alaskan cruise because spending $15,000 feels reckless, even though he has $1.8 million and more income than he needs.

The couple with $2.2 million who drive a 15-year-old car and agonize over whether to upgrade their outdated kitchen because "we don't want to be wasteful."

The tension is real. On one hand, you'll never be this young again. At 65 or 68 or 70, you have energy and health you might not have at 80. The "go-go years" are finite. On the other hand, retirement lasts an unknown number of years. Will it be 10 or 30? How do you know what's safe to spend when you don't know how long the money needs to last? That tension paralyzes people. So they default to what they know: save, be cautious, live below your means.

Except now those instincts work against you.

I recently spoke with a reporter about this. What I told her is what I tell clients: the 85-year-old version of you won't regret the trip you took at 65. At some point, all we have left are memories. We might as well make them while we can.

This is where specialized retirement income expertise becomes valuable. Not to tell you to spend less and be careful, but to show you what you can safely spend. To help you navigate both the numbers and the psychology of this transition.

Someone who can model your specific situation, show you the trade-offs, and help you understand what's possible. Someone who recognizes that the hardest part isn't the math. It's giving yourself permission after decades of discipline telling you to do the opposite.

You didn't save all this money to die with the biggest account balance. You saved it to fund experiences, security, and freedom. Make sure you actually get to use it for that.

## When I Knew It Was Time to Leave

I had another one of those unexplainable moments in 2014.

I'd been working at the large firm for seven years. I'd built a solid client base. I was doing well by their metrics, so well, in fact, I'd just been nominated for *Financial Advisor of the Year*.

Then they decided to reorganize territories. They wanted to move about a third of my clients to a new advisor in another market. Someone with one year of experience, these people had never met.

When I pushed back, the message was clear: "These aren't your clients. They're the firm's clients."

That hit hard. These weren't account numbers to me. They were people who'd trusted me through 2008. People whose retirements I'd helped plan. Relationships built over several years. I couldn't just hand them off. And even if I did, what if they still wanted to work with me? It wasn't like I was moving.

I had countless conversations with my wife, Karen, about what to do. She asked the practical questions. How much would it cost to start a company? Where would we get office space? What about health insurance? Although we had done a great job saving and investing over the years, we still had a mortgage, and it wasn't like the bills were going to stop coming. We were planning to start a family, too. This wasn't a small decision.

But she also asked the most important question. "What do you really think is best for your clients? Should you stay or start your own company?" She was trying to get me to think about the Golden Rule. "How would you want to be served if you were somebody's client?"

There's a saying that a problem well-stated is half-solved. Once she put it that way, I didn't even have to think about what was best. Not for me, but for my clients.

That March, Karen and I took a spring break trip to Cozumel with my parents. My dad had been CFO at the same company for 28 years and was planning to retire soon.

One morning at sunrise, my dad and I were walking on the beach. We were both venting about our situations. I was frustrated with the firm's treatment of my client relationships. He was thinking about what came next after nearly three decades in the same role.

We started talking about starting our own advisory firm. My dad had always wanted to do something like this. As a CFO, people constantly asked him for financial advice. He'd helped countless people informally over the years.

We realized we were saying the same thing. We both wanted to build something different. Something where clients' interests were the priority, where we could help them invest how we invested, and where they were not account numbers on some reorganization spreadsheet.

What's kind of crazy is that conversation happened in March, and by August 1st, I was calling my clients to tell them the news that we had started Stockbridge Private Wealth Management.

Was it scary? Absolutely. Did we have everything figured out? Not even close. But we knew it was time. The same way I'd known driving home after the Katrina flight.

I share this because I want you to understand something: those moments of clarity are real. When you know something needs to change, that instinct deserves to be taken seriously.

And here's what I learned from watching my dad transition into this new chapter: moving *away from* something that's not working is powerful motivation. But you also need something to move *toward*. My dad wasn't just leaving a 28-year career. He was stepping into something he'd always wanted to do. That made all the difference.

Maybe you're feeling something similar about your current advisor. You've worked with them for 15 years. They helped you accumulate wealth. You appreciate that. But something feels off about the advice you're getting for retirement. You're not sure they're equipped for this phase.

Or maybe you're not just moving away from an advisor who lacks retirement income expertise. You're moving toward a retirement you've been working toward for decades, and making sure you have the right guidance for it.

Trust those instincts.

Just like my transition from airline pilot to financial advisor required more than just recognizing it was time to change, your transition into retirement requires more than just recognizing you need different expertise.

You need to act on it.

## What Happens Next

If you've determined you need specialized retirement income expertise, here's what the transition actually looks like.

The logistics are simpler than you think. Accounts transfer electronically through ACATS, the Automated Customer Account Transfer Service. You don't need your current advisor's permission. You don't need to sell anything. Investments stay invested during the move.

You'll meet with the new advisor, discuss your situation, and review their planning process. If it's a good fit and you decide to work together, you'll sign some paperwork, usually electronically now. The new firm initiates the transfer. Within a few days, your accounts appear at the new firm. Your current advisor gets notified by the system.

That's it.

Your specialist will tell you what to bring to the meetings, but typically it's any recent statements from your accounts, your last two years of tax returns, Social Security statements, any pension documents, and estate planning documents if you have them. You can also bring any previous retirement plan documents you want reviewed.

The specialist will show you what comprehensive retirement income planning looks like and help you determine if you're a good fit for each other.

The mechanics are straightforward. The decision is what matters.

## If You're Ready

If you have $500,000 or more in investable assets and you're approaching this transition, I'd welcome a conversation. We work with clients nationwide at Stockbridge Private Wealth Management. This is what we specialize in: helping successful people navigate the shift from accumulation to sustainable retirement income.

Visit www.stockbridgewealth.com or call our office. We'll start with a conversation about your situation. If it makes sense, I'll show you what comprehensive retirement income planning looks like before you make any commitment.

I've created *The Retirement Specialist Selection Checklist* to help you take action. It includes credential verification resources, questions to ask advisors, red flags and green lights, and step-by-step instructions for making a transition if you decide that's right for you.

Download it free at www.stockbridgewealth.com/book

Or use this QR code:

If you'd prefer to find a retirement income specialist in your area, visit The American College's resource at www.youradvisorguide.com to search their directory of RICP professionals. Look for advisors who've invested in the specialized training we've discussed throughout this book.

## Move Forward

The transition moment is real. When it arrives, you'll recognize it.

What matters most is what you do next.

I'm guessing you didn't build your wealth by accident. The time to be purposeful with what's next is now.

Retirement is an opportunity to partner with professionals who understand this phase and are trained to guide it properly. Not to experiment while someone learns on your savings.

You've worked too hard. You've built too much. You deserve better than hope and guesswork.

The wealth you've built isn't just account balances and portfolio statements. It's the experiences you can now afford. The security you've created for yourself and those you love. The freedom you've earned to spend your days as you choose.

Retirement income planning isn't about making your money last. It's about making your life count while you still have the health and energy to live it fully.

What good is financial security without the confidence to actually enjoy it? What value is a well-funded retirement if you spend it worried, cautious, deferring the experiences you worked so hard to make possible?

You didn't save for decades to live small in retirement. You saved to live well.

A good retirement isn't an amount. It's an approach. It's the wisdom to know you've built enough, the courage to actually use what you've created, and the guidance to do so sustainably.

You have the resources. You've earned the opportunity. Now make sure you have the specialized expertise to help you use both wisely.

Move forward with confidence.

Thank you for reading.

## Key Takeaways:

- **Trust the transition moment.** Whether it's recognizing you need specialized expertise, knowing when to retire, or understanding your needs have fundamentally changed, those instinctual moments of clarity are real. They deserve to be acted upon, not ignored.
- **The hardest part isn't the math, it's the mindset.** The discipline that helped you accumulate wealth can become the barrier to enjoying it. You need expertise that understands both the technical side of sustainable withdrawals and the psychological challenge of giving yourself permission to spend after decades of saving.
- **Moving forward requires both "away from" and "towards" motivation.** It's not enough to recognize

that your current situation isn't working. You need clarity about what you're moving toward. That might be a retirement income specialist who can show you what you can safely spend, or simply have the confidence to live the retirement you worked so hard to build.

# About the Author

Eric T. Ludwig, Ph.D., CFP®, RICP®, is co-founder and CEO of Stockbridge Private Wealth Management, a firm dedicated to helping affluent individuals navigate the complex transition from wealth accumulation to life in retirement.

Dr. Ludwig is also Professor of Retirement Income at The American College of Financial Services, where he serves as Director of the Center for Retirement Income and the Retirement Income Certified Professional® (RICP®) designation, the nation's premier credential for retirement specialists.

He holds a doctorate in Personal Financial Planning from Kansas State University and has published research in leading journals. His insights have been featured in *The Wall Street Journal, Time, Forbes, Barron's, Kiplinger's, Money* magazine, and other major national outlets.

Dr. Ludwig is a regular speaker for the largest financial services firms and conferences globally.

He lives in Wisconsin with his wife and daughter.

Website: www.stockbridgwealth.com
LinkedIn: https://www.linkedin.com/in/ericludwigcfp/
Email: ericludwig@stockbridgwealth.com

# Reader Resource

## THE RETIREMENT SPECIALIST SELECTION CHECKLIST

A free companion guide with step-by-step instructions for finding and evaluating retirement income specialists.

https://stockbridgewealth.com/book/

Made in the USA
Monee, IL
16 September 2026

63296742R00122